"*Advertising in the Aging Society* presents a refreshing and rare combination of theory-driven, data-rich research complete with clear implications for advertising practice. After analysis of nearly 3,000 television advertisements, 185 advertising practitioners' survey responses, and 1,834 audience surveys, the authors provide insightful advice regarding the effects, effectiveness, and ethics of portraying 'silver' citizens in advertising. Scholars and practitioners within Japan and beyond will find the research and conclusions to be interesting and valuable. The approach is a model for conducting multi-method research within a cultural context – content, creators, and consumers are all examined within one volume. The book is a first in what should be a growing body of knowledge about our oldest audience."

Michelle R. Nelson, Associate Professor of Advertising, University of Illinois at Urbana-Champaign

"This book, focusing on advertisers and their mature audiences, unpacks the complex relationship between the sources and targets of marketing in a rapidly aging society. That it does so in Japan, a country on the leading edge of this demographic transition, makes it a prescient account of what the remainder of the world might expect. The picture painted by the empirical results is a mixed one – progress is being made but lagging behind the demographic reality of accelerated population aging. These contributions make the book a valuable addition for media, gerontology, and cultural scholars, as well as the purveyors of messages to older consumers."

Merril D. Silverstein, Marjorie Cantor Professor of Aging Studies, Syracuse University

"Japan is the most advanced of rapidly aging societies, but local advertisers seem to have mostly missed the memo. Maybe wisdom really does come with age, for it is commonly accepted that aging consumers have more wealth, leisure time, interest in travel and the wherewithal for romance (and that other thing) than their juniors, yet shallow stereotyping continues in advertising. *Advertising in the Aging Society* is a well-constructed antidote for this marketing myopia, using Japan as the tutorial for other maturing markets, and may well accelerate the careers of those advertising practitioners who open their eyes to the insights within."

Bob Kerwin, former Chairman of Dentsu Young & Rubicam, Tokyo

"The world is changing, and aging. As Prieler and Kohlbacher note, by the year 2050 around 25% of the developed world's population will be over 65. Japan is leading this trend as 'the world's most advanced aging society' and this book is a fascinating study of how advertisers and consumers in Japan are dealing with an aging consumer segment. The lessons learned by marketers and advertisers in Japan, and covered in detail in this book, will lead the rest of the world in shaping how we represent and create messages for the world's most rapidly expanding demographic."

Katherine T. Frith, co-author of Advertising and Societies: Global Issues, *Professor of Advertising, Southern Illinois University*

"*Advertising in the Aging Society* covers a significant topic, since the demographic of older people is increasing around the world and is becoming more crucial as an advertising market. This book skillfully highlights ethical considerations in how to represent older people adequately, and it is one of the few studies that triangulates data from advertising practitioners with content and consumer information."

Jörg Matthes, Director and Professor, Department of
Communication, University of Vienna

"Japan is leading the way in terms of demographic change. Prieler and Kohlbacher are leading the way in terms of academic research on advertising in an aging society. I congratulate them on filling an important gap in the literature on older consumers and advertising research."

George Moschis, Alfred Bernhardt Research Professor of
Marketing and the founding director of the Center for
Mature Consumer Studies (CMCS) at Georgia State University

"This is a very exciting book. Japanese advertising practitioners should listen carefully to Prieler and Kohlbacher's messages. They have implications for advertising around the world as population's aging is a global megatrend."

Setsuo Sakamoto, Executive Producer, Institute of Elder
Knowledge and New Adult Culture, HAKUHODO Inc.

"When I got my first job with an advertising agency, I was told that creating ads was a young man's game. But that was yesterday, a long time ago. In countries with aging populations, how to advertise to older affluent consumers who make up an increasingly large demographic is becoming an urgent priority for advertisers and agencies alike. Nowhere is this more true than in Japan, the world's most rapidly aging society. Michael Prieler and Florian Kohlbacher's *Advertising in the Aging Society: Understanding Representations, Practitioners, and Consumers in Japan* is an indispensable resource for anyone confronting this issue – and not just in Japan."

John McCreery, author of Japanese Consumer Behaviour,
Partner at The Word Works, Ltd.

"Communicating to seniors is a universal challenge that every marketer will face if they haven't done so already. The world grows older every day. So does its population. Japan is testament to that fact, as the most aged society, the very first live case study. The world can learn a lot from what is happening in Japan at the moment and this book admirably demonstrates the issues for marketers."

Aki Kubo, Chairman, Group Representative, Ogilvy & Mather Japan

Advertising in the Aging Society

Understanding Representations, Practitioners, and Consumers in Japan

Michael Prieler
Hallym University, South Korea

and

Florian Kohlbacher
International Business School Suzhou (IBSS), Xi'an Jiaotong-Liverpool University (XJTLU), PR China

palgrave
macmillan

First published 2016 by
PALGRAVE MACMILLAN

Palgrave Macmillan in the UK is an imprint of Macmillan Publishers Limited,
registered in England, company number 785998, of Houndmills, Basingstoke,
Hampshire RG21 6XS.

Palgrave Macmillan in the US is a division of St Martin's Press LLC,
175 Fifth Avenue, New York, NY 10010.

Palgrave Macmillan is the global academic imprint of the above companies
and has companies and representatives throughout the world.

Palgrave® and Macmillan® are registered trademarks in the United States,
the United Kingdom, Europe and other countries.

ISBN: 978–0–230–29339–7

This book is printed on paper suitable for recycling and made from fully
managed and sustained forest sources. Logging, pulping and manufacturing
processes are expected to conform to the environmental regulations of the
country of origin.

A catalogue record for this book is available from the British Library.

Library of Congress Cataloging-in-Publication Data

Prieler, Michael, author.
    Advertising in the aging society : understanding representations,
    practitioners, and consumers in Japan / Michael Prieler, Florian Kohlbacher.
        pages cm
    Includes bibliographical references.
    ISBN 978–0–230–29339–7 (hardback)
        1. Advertising – Japan. 2. Population aging – Japan. 3. Older consumers –
Japan. 4. Consumer behavior – Japan. I. Kohlbacher, Florian, author. II. Title.
HF5813.J3P75 2015
659.1'042—dc 3   2015028738.

I dedicate this book to my parents, Renate and Franz, who introduced me to the beauty of different cultures and taught me to challenge stereotypes and prejudices

Michael

I dedicate this book to my father, Gerhard, "merchant" and entrepreneur, who ignited my passion for studying business and marketing

Florian

Contents

List of Figures

List of Tables

Foreword

Frustration. It's the only word that describes the whole subject of marketing to the world's aging populations. Not with the over-65s of the world themselves. They are a dynamic group of people who are breaking all preconceived rules about what "getting old" means. The frustration has been with my colleagues in the advertising, market research, marketing world, and the journalists who cover it and have been so slow to realize a simple truth: any reasonable analysis of the limited available data suggests that if you want to grow your business in the next few decades then you need to understand the "greys," "silvers," "seniors," "aged," "new life builder," and "old."

I said limited data because it is also true that through combinations of lack of foresight, prejudice, and myths, most organizations have done little real investigation of how to talk to, research, market, and advertise to the 65+ age cohorts that are booming and blooming in so many countries. None more so than Japan. So any new study of how these age groups are represented in advertising is truly welcome.

From 2003 I had the joy of spending a decade leading the Strategy Planning division of McCann Worldgroup in Japan. A joy because the experience of working in the advertising industry in that country is so different and thought-provoking. It did however have its frustrations and to my surprise the aging demographics of the country was perhaps the biggest of them.

To provide some background, I first became interested in aging demographics and its impact on advertising in the late 1980s in my native Sydney. At the time the Australian Bureau of Census issued some reports discussing the potential aging of the population in the twenty-first century. I wrote a summary briefing and distributed it to the management of the McCann offices in Australia who in turn distributed it to clients. The next week I found that it had caused an unexpected stir. One of our clients was a famous manufacturer of toy automobiles who told our account director that they would now need to reconsider their future in the market if the population was going to get old. After all they made toys for kids. Of course we managed to explain that there would be decades before real aging took hold. More importantly I put together a scenario to explain what we now take for granted: an aging population means more living grandparents and a greater ratio of adult relatives for each child which will mean spoiled boys and girls getting more gifts. And that high-end toy cars should do well.

The new One Child Policy in China at that time was to prove that theory correct in that by the late 1990s there were numerous reports of how "kids" categories that took a higher-end approach were doing really well with the "let's spoil our little emperor" scenario. A scenario we were to see repeated as families across many Asian markets began to voluntarily shrink the number of children per family. In a place like Japan, by the turn of the millennium, having just one child, who would be invariably spoiled by doting grandparents and great-grandparents, became the norm.

More importantly the toy car story sparked my real interest in misconceptions about aging populations and what that might mean to advertising and marketing. I was fortunate over the subsequent years to lead a number of research projects across the Asia-Pacific region looking at how different generations reacted to a wide range of issues. In the course of these studies I paid special attention to what I called "New Life Builders," those people aged between their mid-50s and early 70s who were getting close to retirement or had already retired, whose children were leaving or had left home, who unlike their own parents' generation were likely to live for another 20 or 30 years and were realizing they needed to look forward to their future. A big change from the traditional view of retirement as "waiting for death" and a new stage of life for the new and developing middle classes of Asia.

Of course there were clients paying attention. Slowly and quite obviously some marketers started to notice the aging trend: the "usual suspects" of insurers, health service providers, retirement homes. Ask anyone in the industry to this day "which clients are benefiting or targeting the older population" and that is the answer you get.

When I moved to Japan in 2003 I was well aware of it having the oldest demography. I had helped do enough studies to know that the Japanese market was starting to come to grips with knowing it had a "problem" with the possibility of an aging, shrinking population and not many answers. However, I was both surprised and disappointed to find that rather than seeing this as a big opportunity, marketers there were still looking at having a burgeoning older population as a problem. Just like their peers around the world over the previous 40 years, they were focused on "targeting the young" because of misconceptions about developing lifetime loyalty and habits. Misconceptions because the constant change that had happened in Japan in the previous four decades, the constant availability of new products and services, and the fast adaptation the Japanese had made to new technologies had meant change was more a norm than consistency in the behavior of potential consumers of any age. And certainly no less for the about-to-retire.

Think about that. The experience of the typical 60-year-old in Tokyo, Osaka, Fukuoka in 2003 is certainly that of amazingly hard-working, dedicated, and passionate savers. But also the generation that had lived with the rise of SONY, the introduction of the most advanced robot-driven manufacturing, the slickest transport systems, the leading edge of adopting new personal technologies. Forty years of the most advanced convenience stores in the world offering them services you still can't get elsewhere and a constant flow of new products at a rate not matched in any other country. These are people who have spent their whole lives being trained by the world around them to try new products.

Yes, there were Japanese companies actively targeting those over 60. But they were mostly of the usual cohort of industries: insurance, retirement funds and homes, healthcare. Some categories were making an effort in areas such as skincare and cosmetics. But these were more an adjunct of the old approach to aging. Products to "help hide the cracks, grey hair and deterioration of youthful looks." In other words, marketers still saw aging as something to run away from and hide. Or something that meant preparing for a long, slow decline.

That was doubly disappointing. In part because at the same time there was plentiful research indicating that the upcoming retirement of Japan's equivalent to the baby boomer, the *dankai*, would make them healthier, wealthier, and more aware of their potential longevity than previous generations. And in part because they had a different attitude.

A few examples involving music provide a great illustration. In 2006 we were conducting interviews and focus group discussions with men and women who were approaching retirement or had recently retired. Among those men who had retired in recent years – remember at the time the retirement age was 60 – we occasionally heard about their buying or taking up playing instruments and especially guitars again. Subsequently, in 2007, when the first of the *dankai* retired, it was reported that one of the fastest growing categories of sales for the year was again guitars. And in the years that followed there was a lot of reporting about men retiring, getting hold of a guitar, and re-forming bands that in many cases had been dormant since they graduated university: rock bands, cover bands of every genre of pop music popular in their youth in the 1960–1980 period.

Should it be a surprise? Sure, these guys had given up their bands and instruments in their mid-20s to spend three and half decades as dedicated salarymen. However, they had also spent an awful lot of corporate bonding time pursuing their music in the form of karaoke nights. So why should marketers be surprised that this new "aging population" were actually rock 'n' rollers in their hearts?

And for the next couple of decades at least many have money to spend on their passions. The current *dankai* generation who began retiring in 2007 and is tailing off over the next year or so managed to save a lot, and while they do retain a propensity for cautious investment and want to pass on a legacy to their children and grandchildren, they are also more than happy to invest in the present, on enjoying retirement, and the next 30 years of their lives.

I did start to see changes among marketers who realized they had to start talking to this new market. As Tokyo Disneyland put together plans for its 25th anniversary, the key focus was to get people to come back. For two and a half decades just about every family in the country had visited the park as parents and young children. So how to get people to return? What about the grandparents? As young parents they had brought their children a quarter-century ago, so how about getting them to return and relive the experience? Campaigns were developed to encourage grandparents and grandchildren to come together. A different spin on the "toy car" story and the inevitable result of wanting to spoil the one or two grandchildren. But what was surprising was discovering that being re-introduced to Disney led to retired couples visiting on their own, to relive the memories or maybe just to have a little adventure.

We noted too a growing trend for mother/daughter vacations. Adult daughters in their 20s and 30s going on trips with their 50–60-something mothers. A chance to bond, a chance for the daughter to go on a more expensive journey often paid for by the mother, a chance for the mother to go and do something different and live young. A chance to learn from each other. It was a trend that became an important part of planning campaigns for most travel-related companies. It was a theme that we used in campaigns for MasterCard, Cathay Pacific, and others. As this book is published there is much reporting of the success of cruise-liner companies again targeting the *dankai*. We have also seen that where the tradition upon retirement had been that couples would take a short stay in Hawaii, the *dankai* are being more adventurous. They are now looking at destinations for post-retirement vacations spreading all over the world, with more culture and adventure variations and multiple trips being planned and undertaken.

An older generation who actually want to travel and explore.

That signaled a change in mentality.

Further evidence came in the beauty world. Shiseido, Kanebo, and others have had success not by focusing on delivering advertising that said "cover up the problems of aging" but by emphasizing "you can continue to bring out your real beauty." We have seen in recent years more campaigns feature 50-to-70-year-old women who emphasize their continuing vibrant personality as much as their being happy with continuing to express their own ongoing beauty.

Of course "old" people and celebrities had always played a major part in advertising in Japan. The use of the celebrity endorser has always been very common, according to some research the biggest in the world. The image portrayed in *Lost in Translation* by Bill Murray of aged Hollywood stars making gratuitous commercials was and is still true. To this day Audrey Hepburn remains perhaps the most sought-after endorser in the country, decades after her death. However, that too is changing.

Perhaps one of the most successful, and certainly talked about, campaigns of the past ten years has been for BOSS canned coffee and the use of Tommy Lee Jones playing the part of a stony-faced alien come to Earth and somewhat perplexed by the natives. But this was not a case of choosing the actor for his age, or even his fame. Indeed, when the campaign first came to popularity our own research found that among those of all ages who said they liked the advertising less than a third knew the star's name. He was seen as having a "unique face" and character rather than as being an old, well-known endorser.

In the past few years I was fortunate to persuade some clients like Johnson & Johnson to start really investigating the new dynamic of aging. We undertook a number of research studies, often unique in asking people 60–90 years of age to participate. And many of those clients are now actively undertaking the development of new products and marketing campaigns to re-address the Japanese new life builder.

But the frustration remains. Perhaps best summed up by my friend Toru Shibata, ex-president of Johnson & Johnson Consumer Japan, who complains that it is so difficult to talk to his market research suppliers, his advertising agencies, his own marketing departments about targeting 70-year-olds when they are all staffed by people in their 30s and 40s. To those "young" professionals talk of advertising to a 70-year-old seems like talking about their grandmother, or great-grandmother. A beloved relative but a boring and misunderstood target audience.

And that is perhaps why we still see so much stereotyping in advertising use of the older generations. Stereotypes are hard to break. Getting marketers and their agencies to rethink the opportunities is hard. For example, understanding that rather than products and images "to help the feeble" it might be better to suggest that those same products that are good for those in their golden years are good for all is a concept slow to get started but with unlimited potential.

With all that said, it is such a pleasure to have helped in a small way with the project and knowledge in this volume. As mentioned above, the amount of research into the habits, the beliefs, and the actual representation of older Japan, and older populations anywhere, in marketing communications is very thin. It is only in the past few years that national polls, tracking studies, and any form of general research even asked people over 60 to take part. As such, any addition to our understanding is a big gain.

I began by describing my frustration; let me end with hope. Japan is in a unique situation. Having the "oldest" demography on the planet it has the opportunity to lead the world in the understanding of how to incorporate an aging population into its active society, how to market to it, how to rethink the messaging that today's modern retiree will find attractive. Personally I have long advocated that the aging population is Japan's biggest opportunity. Let's look forward to great marketing communication taking advantage of that possibility.

Dave McCaughan
(Previously Director of Strategic Planning,
McCann Worldgroup Asia-Pacific)
Thought Leader & Storyteller at Bibliosexual www.bibliosexual.com

Preface

This book consists of a total of six chapters and three appendices. We have tried to write the chapters in a way that they can be read independently of one another and in any given order preferred by the reader without comprising too much on understandability. The order that we have chosen is the most natural one. The empirical Chapters 3, 4, and 5 build on a background provided by Chapters 1 and 2, while Chapter 6 is a synopsis of our conclusions from the research. Finally, for those readers who would like to know more about how the research was actually done, we explain the method in detail in Appendices 1–3. What follows now is a brief outline of Chapters 1–6.

Chapter 1 is structured along the lines of the reasons and motivations for the book. In the first part of Chapter 1 we provide an overview of aging populations around the world and how they affect societies and businesses. The second part of this chapter discusses what challenges and opportunities marketers and advertising practitioners face in this changing marketplace in Japan and shows that Japan can be an excellent case study for other countries that could potentially experience similar developments in the future. In the third part of this chapter we introduce the most common sources of information for older people and then specifically highlight the importance of mass media and advertising in those populations. This is followed by an overview of how the media affects consumer socialization and socialization in general, and thus how it might affect attitudes toward older people. At the end of this chapter we discuss explicitly attitudes toward older people in society, with a special focus on Japan.

Chapter 2 gives a short introduction to Japanese advertising (including advertising agencies, advertising media, and television advertisements) and then explains and discusses some of the so-called specialties of Japanese television advertising, including soft-sell advertisements, 15-second advertisements, lack of comparative advertising, advertisements with celebrities, and advertisements with foreigners. We conclude that most of these "specialties" are actually myths lacking in empirical evidence and are not unique to Japan. In short, this chapter debunks the myths about Japanese advertising and shows that cultural explanations are not sufficient in and of themselves; it is necessary to take factors other than culture into account, as other countries have similar advertising characteristics, and there are also business/economic reasons for some of these "specialties" at work.

Chapter 3 presents the results of a content analysis on the representation of older people in Japanese television advertisements. We show that there were several changes in Japanese advertising between 1997 and 2007 that may reflect the increasing importance of older people within Japanese society, such as increasing appearances of older people, increased instances where older people were featured alone and in major roles, and where older people were portrayed in more favorable ways, which suggests that their status changed. However, some aspects have remained unchanged; older people continue to be underrepresented, which does not reflect demographic reality, and are used in advertisements for foods and beverages, confirming findings from previous studies. Our findings indicate that the representation of older people in Japanese television advertising has changed but remains unrealistic.

Chapter 4 looks at advertising practitioners' views on the use of older models in advertising in Japan and thus their opinions on such representations. We have found that the interest by companies in using older models in advertising is going to increase over the coming years and so will the amount of older models. In addition, older models may be effective in achieving communications objectives (depending on the purpose, product category, and target group) and in aiding persuasion through mood and enhanced source credibility. When targeting an older audience, older models may be particularly effective for health-related products and when targeting a general audience for the financial services/insurance product category. Generally, older models were found to be more effective for age-oriented product categories than for youth-oriented ones. Last but not least, older spokespersons may be more effective targeting an older audience than a general audience when they are aged 50–64 than when they are aged 65 years or older.

Chapter 5 presents the results of a large sample survey of older consumers' advertising usage and response to the portrayal of older people in television advertising. We found that older consumers rely to a fair amount on advertising as an information source in making purchase decisions. In terms of their responses to the portrayal of older people in television advertising, older consumers perceive the portrayal of older people in Japanese television advertisements as stereotypical/inaccurate and partly negative, though not necessarily as insulting. Last but not least, older Japanese consumers have the intention not to purchase a product if its advertising is perceived as portraying older people negatively, that is, they are willing to boycott these products and/or the company (and its other products). These findings were not limited to older consumers, but also younger consumers (20–49 years of age), who gave similar responses.

Chapter 6 summarizes our research by offering conclusions based on the empirical research presented in Chapters 3, 4, and 5. Our research shows that older people are highly underrepresented (especially women) and are portrayed in stereotypical, albeit not necessarily unfavorable, ways. This is despite the fact that advertising practitioners have a generally positive view toward using older models, even though only for an older target audience. Finally, both younger and older consumers perceive the representation of older people in advertising as stereotypical and partly negative, and are willing to boycott companies negatively portraying older people. After discussing possible reasons for these long-standing stereotypes and their possible effects on the audience, the chapter closes by questioning whether advertising regulation related to portrayals of older people might be necessary in the future.

We now invite you to enjoy reading the book *Advertising in the Aging Society*, and please remember: No matter whether you are young, middle-aged, or old at this moment, we are all aging in the meantime.

Michael Prieler, Chuncheon, South Korea
Florian Kohlbacher, Suzhou, PR China
July 2015

Acknowledgments

First and foremost we would like to thank Professor Shigeru Hagiwara and Professor Florian Coulmas. Hagiwara-sensei was the deputy director of the Institute for Media and Communications Research at Keio University in Tokyo when the project started in 2007, and he was a very important member of our project team until his retirement in 2013. Coulmas-sensei was the director of the German Institute for Japanese Studies (DIJ) Tokyo; he was Florian's boss from 2007 to 2014 and Michael's boss from 2007 to 2009. Without the wholehearted support of both of them this project would never have been possible. We would also like to thank Professor Akie Arima for her support, especially in the initial stage of the project, and our research assistants, Yoh Murayama and Yuko Shiki. Yuko Horiuchi's help in conducting the advertising agency survey was invaluable, as was her continual advice on issues about the older people's market in Japan. Professor Clemens Tesch-Römer has given us invaluable feedback on our content analysis. Professors Wolfgang Jagodzinski and Emmanuel Chéron have on numerous occasions provided advice on statistical matters. In addition, we would like to thank Dave McCaughan, Todd Holden, Cornelius Herstatt, and the advertising agencies Dentsu, Hakuhodo, McCann-Erickson, and Asatsu-DK for their support through numerous discussions related to advertising in the aging society. Last but not least, we would like to thank the Yoshida Hideo Memorial Foundation for supporting this project from 2008 to 2010. All errors and omissions in the project are solely ours.

On a more personal note, we would like to thank our wives, Cherry and Makiko, and our families for their support and patience during the many evenings and weekends we spent finishing this book.

Michael dedicates this book to his parents, Renate and Franz, who have supported him in all life circumstances, introduced him to the beauty of different cultures, and taught him to challenge stereotypes and prejudices. They are the perfect example that age is just a number, and their never-ending curiosity, activeness, and open-mindedness are the best proof that stereotypes of older people are often inaccurate.

Florian dedicates this book to his father, Gerhard,[1] the "merchant" and entrepreneur who ignited his passion for studying business and marketing and who provides constant support and advice on all matters in life. Gerhard is another great example that age is just a number, having become father for a second time at age 54 and having started his own business at age 60. A picture showing him as a "young" father at around age 60 has been tremendously helpful for Florian in educating many marketing and advertising practitioners during talks and seminars.

Note

1. Florian dedicated his first book, *International Marketing in the Network Economy: A Knowledge-Based Approach*, 2007, Palgrave Macmillan, to his mother Annemarie, so it is now his father's turn. But of course Annemarie deserves a big "thank you" here as well!

1
Advertising in the Aging Society: Setting the Stage

The motivation for this book is grounded in several reasons. First, older people are of interest in our study because of their rapid increase around the world and specifically in Japanese society, as well as their increasing importance as a market segment (Coulmas, 2007; Kohlbacher & Herstatt, 2011). Siano and associates (2013) argue that "Understanding corporate communication strategy takes on critical importance whenever organisations are threatened by environmental changes ... that lead to the redefinition of the role of the organisation in relation to its key stakeholders" (p. 151). Demographic change is such an environmental change that requires responses from corporations (Kohlbacher & Matsuno, 2012). Second, mass media in general and television in particular rank prominently among the major sources of information among older people and are tapped for purchasing and consumption decisions (Kohlbacher, Prieler, & Hagiwara, 2011a; Lumpkin & Festervand, 1988; Phillips & Sternthal, 1977; Smith, Moschis, & Moore, 1985). Third, research around the globe (including Japan) on the representation of older people in television advertising finds them to be underrepresented (Prieler, Kohlbacher, Hagiwara, & Arima, 2015; Simcock & Sudbury, 2006; Y. B. Zhang et al., 2006) and sometimes even to be portrayed negatively or stereotypically (Prieler, Kohlbacher, Hagiwara, & Arima, 2011a; Zhou & Chen, 1992). Such representation has an impact on individual and societal attitudes and perceptions toward older people (Bandura, 2009; Gerbner, 1998; Morgan, Shanahan, & Signorielli,

2009; Pollay, 1986; Shrum, Wyer Jr., & O'Guinn, 1998) as well as toward their consumer behavior (Ferle & Lee, 2003; Moschis, 1987). Last but not least, empirical research on practitioner views/consumer responses to representations of older people is scarce and was conducted many years ago in different cultural contexts (e.g., Festervand & Lumpkin, 1985; Greco, 1988, 1989; Kolbe & Burnett, 1992; Langmeyer, 1984; Szmigin & Carrigan, 2000a). In addition, while there are numerous guides on how to market and target to older people (e.g., Moschis, 1994, 1996; Nyren, 2007; Stroud, 2005; Stroud & Walker, 2013; Tréguer, 2002), there is comparatively little research on the cultural and ethical considerations in using older people in advertising and the media (Featherstone & Wernick, 1995; Harrington, Bielby, & Bardo, 2014; Harwood, 2007; Ylänne, 2012).

This chapter is structured along the lines of the reasons and motivations for the book. In the first part of the chapter, we provide an overview of aging societies around the world and how they affect societies and businesses. The second part of this chapter discusses what challenges and opportunities marketers and advertising practitioners face in this changing marketplace in Japan and shows that Japan can be an excellent case study for other countries that could potentially experience similar developments in the future. In the third part of this chapter we introduce the most common sources of information for older people and then specifically highlight the importance of mass media and advertising in those populations. This is followed by an overview of how the media affects consumer socialization and socialization in general, and thus how it might affect attitudes toward older people. At the end of this chapter, we will discuss explicitly attitudes toward older people in society, with a special focus on Japan.

Aging societies around the world

Population aging on a global scale

Demographic change has emerged as a powerful megatrend affecting a large number of countries around the world. This aging, and in some cases shrinking, of the population has vast overall economic, social, individual, and organizational consequences (Drucker, 2002;

Dychtwald & Flower, 1990; Harper, 2014; Kohlbacher & Herstatt, 2011; Magnus, 2009).

Globally, the number of people aged 65 or over is expected almost to triple, increasing from 530 million in 2010 to 1.5 billion by 2050. In the more developed regions, 16% of the population is already aged 65 years or over and that proportion is projected to reach 25.8% in 2050 (see Figure 1.1). In developed countries as a whole, the number of older people has already equaled the number of children (people under age 15), and by 2050 the number of older people in developed countries will be more than the number of children (25.8% vs. 16.1%). But this trend is not restricted to the developed world. In developing countries as a whole, even though just 5.8% of the population is today aged 65 years or over, that proportion will more than double by 2050, reaching 14.0% that year and 21.0% in 2100 (United Nations Population Division, 2012). We assume these unprecedented trends to heavily affect societies, companies, and politics. We further expect this development to be relevant for industrialized nations as well as for certain emerging economies where aging societies also become an increasingly important issue (Antony, Purwar, Kinra, & Moorthy, 2011; Sasat & Bowers, 2013; N. J. Zhang, Guo, & Zheng, 2012).

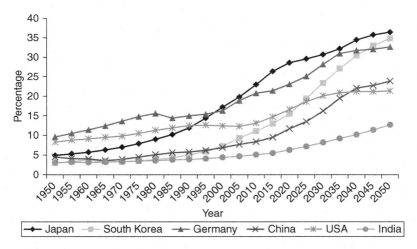

Figure 1.1   Percentage of population age 65 or over (middle variant).
Source: Based on the 2012 Population Database of the UN Population Division (2012).

Business implications of the aging society

Against this backdrop, it is all the more surprising to see that research on the implications of the demographic change on societies, industries, and companies is still in its infancy. Most accounts of the so-called demographic "problem" deal, as the term already suggests, with the challenges and threats of the demographic development. These discussions feature, for example, the shrinking workforce, welfare effects, and social conflicts. Academic literature on management is only slowly taking up this challenge, with recent editorials and feature articles calling for more research (Chand & Tung, 2014; Kulik, Ryan, Harper, & George, 2014). In particular, empirically grounded work is missing.

We need to know how companies and whole industries are coping with demographic change. We need to know what the needs of older people are compared to other age groups, and we need to look for practical solutions to their needs. There is also a lack of concepts, processes, and practical solutions in various fields and functions of management: How to segment and approach the market for older people? How to adapt product development, design, and delivery of value to this market? How to grasp the latent needs and wants of the potential older customers? (Kohlbacher, 2011; Kohlbacher, Gudorf, & Herstatt, 2011).

Chances and opportunities are often neglected in the context of demographic change. The emergence of new markets, the potential for innovations, the integration of older people into jobs and workplaces, the joy of active aging, and the varied roles of older people within society are just a few examples of how what at first sight appears to be a crisis could be turned into an opportunity (Kohlbacher, Herstatt, & Levsen, 2015; McCaughan, 2015; Nyren, 2007). All in all, countries and industries are reacting very differently – from still neglecting to proactively looking for and developing solutions (Kohlbacher, 2011; Kohlbacher, Gudorf et al., 2011).

Peter Drucker wrote about the business implications of demographic change as early as 1951 and has repeatedly stressed their importance (Drucker, 1951, 2002). One particularly essential implication of the demographic change is the emergence and constant growth of the "silver market" (Kohlbacher & Herstatt, 2011), the market segment more or less broadly defined as those people aged 50 or 55 and older.

Increasing in number and share of the total population while at the same time being relatively well-off, this market segment can be seen as very attractive and promising, although still very underdeveloped in terms of product and service offerings (Kohlbacher, 2011; Kohlbacher, Gudorf et al., 2011).

Marketing scholars already debated the marketing opportunities of the older segment in the 1960s (Goldstein, 1968; Reinecke, 1964). However, despite the growing importance of the older population, older consumers are still under-researched and often not included in a range of marketing and advertising practices (Bartos, 1980; Gunter, 1998; Moschis, 2003, 2012; Sudbury & Simcock, 2009b). This is in contrast to the growing body of research on older consumers' behavior (Barnhart & Peñaloza, 2013; Lambert-Pandraud & Laurent, 2010; Lambert-Pandraud, Laurent, & Lapersonne, 2005) which provides evidence of age and cohort differences in consumption and suggests that marketers should respond to these accordingly. While executives generally seem to acknowledge the importance of demographic trends, relatively few companies take concrete action to try to develop the older market segment (Economist Intelligence Unit, 2011; Kohlbacher, 2011; Stroud & Walker, 2013) although there are a few notable exceptions (Chand & Tung, 2014; Kohlbacher et al., 2015).

Japan's aging society

The world's most aged society

The vast majority of the research on older consumers has been conducted in North America and Europe (Kohlbacher & Chéron, 2012), while Japan, the country most severely affected by demographic change, with a rapidly aging as well as shrinking population (Coulmas, 2007; Coulmas, Conrad, & Schad-Seifert, 2008; Muramatsu & Akiyama, 2011), has been largely neglected. This is astonishing given that older people in Japan hold a disproportionately large amount of personal financial assets. Thus, older people form an attractive market potential. As a consequence, the major Japanese advertising agencies have even set up specialized departments to study older consumers (Dentsu Senior Project, 2007; Hakuhodo Elder Business Suishinshitsu, 2006).

With 26% of its population at 65+ in 2014 (Statistics Japan, 2014b), Japan is the most advanced aging society in the world today, and 87% of Japanese acknowledge aging to be a problem (Pew Research Center, 2014). Japan became an aged society in 1994 – sooner than other industrial nations – when its share of older citizens exceeded 14%. Japan's share of people over 64 reached 21% in 2007, making it the first country to be labeled a super-aged or hyper-aged society (Coulmas, 2007). As Japan was the first society to experience such dramatic demographic change, its companies were the first to be affected by its consequences and had to adapt their strategies, product lines, and advertising to these new challenges early on.

Predictions indicate that nearly one-third of all Japanese people will be over 64 by 2030 (United Nations Population Division, 2012). At present, 29.0% of women are 65 and older, while the corresponding percentage for men is 23.2% (Statistics Japan, 2014b). Overall, the ratio between the 65+ population and the total population is the highest in Japan, and is forecast to continue increasing and to remain ahead of the rest of the world. No other country has ever experienced such rapid population aging (Clark, Ogawa, Kondo, & Matsukura, 2010).

Shifting markets

Demographic change will also shift market segments. A declining youth segment can be anticipated, in contrast with the continuously growing segment of older people (Kohlbacher, 2011; Kohlbacher & Herstatt, 2011). In fact, many market participants are concerned about the shrinking customer base of young, dynamic buyers as well as the demands of an older target group which are still not very well understood. Demographic change could therefore cause problems for companies that do not adjust their product range and do not address new target groups.

The number of potential customers is not the sole determinant of new business opportunities. Purchasing power and consumer behavior play a significant role and could compensate for the decline in customer numbers (Kohlbacher, 2011). Older people tend to spend their accumulated income and wealth instead of concentrating on savings and investments. Japanese private households with heads aged 50+ spend considerably more money per head than the younger age groups (see Figure 1.2).

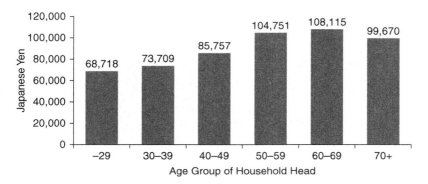

Figure 1.2 Average monthly consumption expenditures per household (by age group of the household head in Japanese yen, 2013 – average spending for one person in two-or-more-person households)

Source: Authors' calculations based on Statistics Japan, 2013.

Older people's high purchasing power also stems from their financial wealth. On average, Japanese households with heads aged 60+ have savings of about 20 million yen. Older people are therefore the top age group in terms of savings. Per person, the generation of people over 70 has savings of more than 10 million yen, closely followed by 60-to-69-year-olds, with 9.1 million yen (see Figure 1.3). As a matter of fact, older people hold a disproportionately large amount of personal financial assets, with those in their 50s and 60s owning 21% and 31% respectively of the total, and those aged 70+ holding 28%. This means that people aged 50+ hold about 80% of the total personal financial assets in Japan (Nikkei Weekly, 2010). Furthermore, the older Japanese generally have nearly no debt and own the property where they live. However, this does not apply to all of Japan's older people, and the number of poorer older people is expected to rise in the future (Fukawa, 2008; Kohlbacher & Weihrauch, 2009).

Thus the market for older people is seen as a very lucrative market segment. The main focus, at the moment, is on the "old, rich, and healthy"; the "old, poor, and sick" are receiving significantly less attention. There are signs that the market for older people of the future is going to look completely different and that the group of the "old, poor, and sick" could form a clear majority due to: (1) increasing social stratification in general, including issues of precariousness and a widening gap between rich and poor (key word: *kakusa*

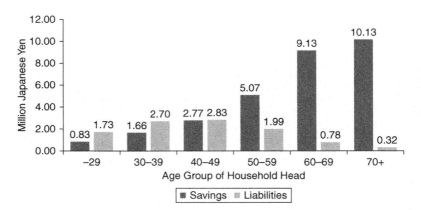

Figure 1.3   Average savings and liabilities held per household (by age group of household head in million yen, 2014 – average for one person in household)
Source: Authors' calculations based on Statistics Japan, 2014a.

shakai = gap society; see for details Hommerich, 2012; Kingston, 2013); (2) the increasing number of people aged 75 and over (this is the age after which physical decline is said to accelerate considerably, and since November 2007 this segment accounts for more than 10% of the Japanese population); and (3) the high number of non-regular employees with insufficient social security (more than one-third of all employees in Japan). As a matter of fact, income and economic inequality as well as poverty among older people are issues of rising concern in Japan (Fukawa, 2008; Ohtake, 2008; Shirahase, 2008). This could become a demographic time bomb and leads to the question of a corporate social responsibility to provide products and services that support seniors in their everyday lives and enable them to grow old in a humane way. Given the right business model, socially and ethically responsible action can also yield economically responsible profits (Kohlbacher & Weihrauch, 2009), not to mention positive reputational effects (see also Kohlbacher, 2011). In this book we focus of course on the current cohorts of older people, but here as well, important implications for corporate social responsibility and marketing ethics can be identified (see also Chapter 6).

Segmenting the market for older people

Definitions of the market for older people, the "silver market," or the "growth market age" vary significantly; it includes people older than 49 or 54 years of age (generation 50+ or 55+) – however, these definitions also include age groups up to the age of 90 to 100. That is, included in this segment are both age groups younger than the baby boomers as well as age groups that are older. While Japan also has adopted the World Health Organization's definition of "older person" (*kōreisha* in Japanese) as 65 years or older, this definition was extended to the 50–64 age segment (called *shinia* = senior in Japanese) by Japanese advertising agencies (Dentsu Senior Project, 2007; Hakuhodo Elder Business Suishinshitsu, 2006) based on the importance of the baby boom generation (*dankai sedai*: those born between 1947–1949 or 1951 in Japan) who were in their 50s at that time. We have followed in this book this more inclusive definition of older people which is used by Japanese advertising agencies. The 50+ definition is also commonly used in academic advertising and marketing research and in business practices, both in Japan and other countries, though it is by no means a homogeneous market segment (Carrigan & Szmigin, 2000b; Yoon & Powell, 2012).

In order to acknowledge possible differences between the 50–64 and the 65+ age group, we have followed the accepted way of splitting our samples into these age groups. This was confirmed by publications of major Japanese agencies (Dentsu Senior Project, 2007; Hakuhodo, 2003), our interviews and the pre-test, as well as marketing research in Japan (Kohlbacher & Chéron, 2012; Murata, 2012). In many cases, 65 also marks the time of transition into retirement, an important phase in a person's life, which also makes itself useful for segmentation purposes (Burnett, 1989; Kohlbacher, 2011). Indeed, given that scholars have frequently pointed to the fact that older people might not form one homogeneous market segment (e.g., Gwinner & Stephens, 2001; Kohlbacher & Chéron, 2012; Moschis, 1996; Sudbury & Simcock, 2009a), it is an important contribution of our research to distinguish between the younger and the older part of this market.

Currently the business world in Japan is highly attentive to the baby boomer generation, which represents the most important group of older customers (Dentsu Senior Project, 2007). The baby boomers have always been highly active, energetic, consumption-oriented, and formed a wealthy subgroup, being curious about technological innovations and having a shopping-related mentality (McCreery, 2000). Along with retirement comes newly gained free time. This is the reason why the baby boomer generation, which has high purchasing power and propensity to consume, is a very attractive potential target group for companies in the market for older people (Kohlbacher, 2011; Sekizawa, 2008). Moreover, older people tend to spend their accumulated income and wealth instead of concentrating on savings and investments.

The market for older people – due to its wide age range – is by no means a homogeneous market (Kohlbacher, 2011; Kohlbacher & Chéron, 2012). Accessing the market appropriately therefore requires a consideration of not only cohort-specific behavior, but also of age-specific preferences. To exclusively define the target group according to age is insufficient because the biological age of people does not reveal much about their performance and activity-related condition, nor about their individual predispositions, needs, and preferences (Moschis, 1994, 2012). Thus, several other segmentation approaches were applied (McCaughan, 2015; Moschis, Lee, & Mathur, 1997; Sudbury & Simcock, 2009a). Generally, most older people tend to feel ten years younger than they actually are or tend to identify themselves strongly with people ten years younger than themselves (Barak, 2009; Sudbury-Riley, Kohlbacher, & Hofmeister, 2015). This situation was also found in Japan (Kohlbacher & Chéron, 2012; Sudbury-Riley et al., 2015; Van Auken & Barry, 2009). The phenomenon of a young cognitive age is especially important when trying to appeal to the target group of older people (Stephens, 1991; Szmigin & Carrigan, 2000b; Van Auken & Barry, 2009).

Another way of segmenting the market for older people is based on life events (Moschis, 2007, 2012). One such event is retirement. Leaving work and starting retirement represents a break, so that the market for older people can be split, regardless of age, into the groups of "pre-retirement" and "post-retirement." The wants and needs of older people are comparably diverse and the areas and industry sectors that feed the market for older people can also profit from this development. At first only the healthcare sector was expected to profit due to the rising demand for medical treatment and healthcare services, but the high number of aged wealthy people, especially in the baby boomer generation, and their favorable spending behavior, soon focused attention on the opportunities in other sectors. The advent of a new, affluent older customer segment was considered to contribute to the creation of a new and lucrative market for older people beyond the medical industry (Kohlbacher, 2011).

Various Japanese companies have successfully created demand among this target group, thus turning a potential threat into an opportunity. However, these are only pioneering efforts (Kohlbacher, 2011; Kohlbacher, Gudorf et al., 2011). Many companies are caught up in old patterns and risk shrinking sales unless they also target older customers. Even though most of the evidence is anecdotal, the number of Japanese companies developing products for the market for older people remains low.

The market for older people, or "silver market" can be roughly divided into the following three sub-segments (Kohlbacher, 2011):

1. *Easy-to-operate and easy-to-use products.* A classic example in the Japanese market is the "Raku-Raku" phone, a mobile phone with easy-to-read fonts, larger-sized keyboard, less complex functions and simple and intuitive operation. Its noise-detection system, which automatically adjusts the volume of the other caller's voice according to the surrounding noise level and suppresses background noise, ensures that the user's voice is transmitted clearly (Kohlbacher & Hideg, 2011).

2. *Luxury goods for wealthy older people.* These products are not exclusively or necessarily age-related. Older customers need the same or similar products and services as other age groups. Because of their financial position as well as the increased time they have to shop after retirement, it is possible to specifically attract this customer group. Successful examples are (group) travel and yachts as well as retro-products such as electric guitars and certain types of motorcycles. In general, Japanese companies assume that older consumers will eventually have higher expectations with respect to product design, quality, and services, and they offer products and services accordingly.

3. *"Gerontechnology" or support and care devices for older people with disabilities or limited mobility.* Due to the increasing number of older people and the growing needs for older people, gerontechnological devices are important products for older people, and at the same time they can be used by younger patients. Special growth areas are household robots as well as the health care and nursing sector. The automobile industry has also adjusted to the constantly growing number of older drivers with "silver cars."

Other segments in the Japanese market for older people which are often seen as being very promising: cosmetics, nutrition products, hobby equipment, household appliances, home accessories, clothing, financial and insurance products, and continued education. A further important area includes retro-products (Coulmas, 2007; Kohlbacher, 2011).

Regarding the market for older people and its age-specific segmentation, it is important to note that successful new products oriented to the needs of older people are not restricted to use by older people. Practical, helpful, and easy-to-use products offer additional value for all consumers, regardless of age. For this reason, new products that are not related to age – that is, universal – can be used effectively and successfully by young and not-so-young customers alike. In this context, key words like "ageless marketing" or "age-neutral marketing" (Stroud, 2005; Wolfe & Snyder, 2003), "universal design" as well as "transgenerational design" (Pirkl, 1994, 2011), play a key role. Universally designed products should be usable by everyone regardless of age, including people with age-related restrictions, but they should be so without emphasizing this aspect to avoid putting off younger customers. An interesting example of a transgenerational product is Nintendo's hugely successful Wii game console which deliberately seeks to bring several generations together through common games and therefore makes it appealing to the whole family, even grandparents. In addition, games are available that are designed to keep older people – as well as younger people – physically and mentally fit (Kohlbacher, 2011; Kohlbacher & Hang, 2011).

The Japanese lead market

The speed and intensity of Japan's demographic change and the resulting shift in market segments and demand structure are among the reasons why Japan is often considered the forerunner in the market for older people. Besides the country's demographic development, researchers have also pointed to the peculiar Japanese consumer behavior and the innovative capacity of Japanese companies (Kohlbacher, 2011; Kohlbacher, Gudorf et al., 2011; Kohlbacher, Herstatt, & Schweisfurth, 2011). Japanese customers have generally been considered as very quality-oriented and therefore demanding. This characteristic is considered especially true for older customers, given their life experience and financial resources. High quality and excellent service are therefore indispensable for reaching wealthy Japanese customers. Japanese consumers also have a greater openness to technological novelties compared to other countries.

Being engaged in a rapidly aging market like Japan provides the chance to learn early from successful examples and solutions, and apply them to the global market situation. Demographic change reflects a global trend affecting not only most of the industrialized nations, but also several of the emerging markets. Indeed, the experiences encountered in the Japanese "lead market" may provide not only valuable insights into the societal implications of demographic change but may also uncover trends, opportunities, and innovative approaches for markets and advertising in other countries (Kohlbacher, Gudorf et al., 2011; Kohlbacher & Rabe, 2015).

According to Clark and associates (2010), "a careful assessment of the impact of population decline and rapid aging in Japan can provide insights and important lessons for the future of Europe and other developed countries" (p. 208) as it is at the forefront of the demographic transition (Muramatsu & Akiyama, 2011). Indeed, it has often been argued that Japan is playing a pioneering role in the market for older people, and can thus be regarded as a lead market (Coulmas, 2007; Kohlbacher, Gudorf et al., 2011; Kohlbacher & Herstatt, 2008; Kohlbacher, Herstatt et al., 2011; Kohlbacher & Rabe, 2015) which can also teach us potential lessons on how to best advertise to older people.

While the previous sections have given an overview of the aging society and its influence on marketing and advertising, the following sections will give an overview of the information sources and media older people are using. This will be followed by explaining the possible effects of media exposure, including shaping attitudes toward older people.

Information sources, media effects, and attitudes toward older people

Information sources for older people

In the process of aging, people undergo gradual social, psychological, and physical changes that ultimately affect the type of information to which they are exposed (Phillips & Sternthal, 1977). This is why older consumers have been reported to differ from their younger counterparts in terms of the information sources they use (Bernhardt & Kinnear, 1976) and the scope and intensity of their information searches (Laroche, Cleveland, & Browne, 2004). One of the first studies on the sources of information for older people was conducted by Schiffman (1971), who suggested that internal information in the form of past experience "may supplement or even serve as a substitute for external sources of information" (p. 35). However, his results also indicate that both external and internal sources of information affect older consumers' decisions to try a new product (Schiffman, 1971). Klippel and Sweeney (1974) found that informal sources of information (friends, neighbors, family, etc.) are more important to older consumers than formal ones (e.g., advertisements in different media) and that this applies across a broad product spectrum. Their research also revealed, however, that the reliance on informal or formal sources of information also depends on whether the consumers are internally or externally oriented. The "externals" believe that forces outside their control dominate their reinforcements, placing more importance on informal information sources than the "internals" (Klippel & Sweeney, 1974). In contrast, Philips and Sternthal (1977) stressed the importance of formal information sources (i.e., the mass media) for the older consumer. They hypothesized that older consumers would have greater exposure to and reliance on mass media sources of information than their younger counterparts due to the attrition in life space and reduced activity level that accompanies advancing age (Phillips & Sternthal, 1977).

Results from a study by Festervand and Lumpkin (1985) indicate that as for mass media exposure, older consumer are exposed primarily to television and newspapers, which are preferred over radio and magazines as sources of general and purchase-specific information. Overall, the findings showed that many older consumers do not consider advertising to be a good source of purchase-specific information, primarily due to a perceived lack of credibility and the inaccurate portrayal of older people in advertisements (Festervand & Lumpkin, 1985). Mason and Bearden's (1978) research revealed that while older consumers indeed rely heavily on personal experience and advice of friends, relatives, and others for their purchasing decisions, they are at the same time "prodigious consumers of mass media" (p. 456). In another empirical study on the purchase information sources of older people, Lumpkin and Festervand (1988) found that older people did not use experience, family, friends, and neighbors to the extent suggested by previous research. Additionally, their results indicated that older people utilize mass media sources as well as salespeople and independent sources more than non-older people. In an empirical study on the perception of television advertisements by older viewers, Schreiber and Boyd (1980) found that the majority of respondents felt that television advertisements provide them with useful sources of information, while only 28% judged the information in television advertisements to be useless to them. However, 63% of their respondents saw television advertisements as "often" or "always" confusing (Schreiber & Boyd, 1980). Smith and associates (1985) found that even though older consumers may not necessarily be exposed to more advertising, they rely more on mass media advertising as they age. They also revealed that there is less interaction with friends and family, and, as a result, less reliance on such sources of consumer information among older consumers (Smith et al., 1985). In contrast, Mathur (1999) found in his study on the adoption of technological innovation by older people that family members play an especially important role as an information source. Similarly, Patterson (2007) showed that personal sources, such as family and friends, are the most important sources of information in regard to travel destinations, but magazines, newspapers, and television documentaries also play some role. In sum, empirical evidence as to which type of information source is more important is rather inconclusive and there seem to be inconsistent patterns of media usage across segments of older consumers (B. Davis & French, 1989; Lumpkin & Festervand, 1988). In addition, the preferred information source and ad usage might also depend on the product type (Strutton & Lumpkin, 1992) and the income or affluence of the consumer (Burnett, 1991).

Mass media and advertising

Mass media and advertising play an important role in informing purchasing decisions of older consumers. While the Internet has also become more important for older people (Hesse et al., 2005; Hilt & Lipschultz, 2004; Taha, Sharit, & Czaja, 2009), mass media has frequently been reported to feature prominently in older people's lives, and they have a strong preference for informational content while still wanting to be entertained when using the media (Gunter, 1998; J. D. Robinson, Skill, & Turner, 2004). Among the various mass media, television viewing is a favorite pastime, and older people watch more television than other age groups; furthermore, they watch programs that provide information at higher rates than do younger adults (Gunter, 1998; Harwood, 2007; Nussbaum, Pecchioni, Robinson, & Thompson, 2000; J. D. Robinson et al., 2004).

This is true in Japan, where no other medium is consumed as frequently and by so many people as television, especially by older cohorts (Shiraishi, 2008). Daily use of television is reported by 89.8% of the Japanese population, followed by 62.7% for newspapers (Nihon Shimbun Kyokai, 2010). A TV set can be found in nearly 100% of Japanese households. In 2005, the average daily television viewing time was 3 hours 43 minutes. Men in the 50–59 age group watch less than average at only 3 hours 23 minutes per day, while all other older-age groups watch more TV than other age groups in Japan. Women in the 50–59 age group watch 4 hours 6 minutes of TV daily, and women over the age of 60 even more at 5 hours per day. Men in the latter age group overtake their female counterparts, watching 5 hours 21 minutes per day (Shiraishi, 2008).

Television advertising holds the biggest share (66.5%) of the mass communications advertising budget (based on Dentsu, 2015). The Japanese population also has the most contact with television advertising (92.9%), followed by newspapers (84.2%), and magazines (63.6%). While newspaper advertisements have an older audience and Internet advertisements are targeted at a younger viewer, television advertising is popular across all age groups (Nihon Shimbun Kyokai, 2010). Television, then, is the advertising form with the broadest influence, particularly because it is the easiest to understand, the most entertaining, and the most spoken about with other people (Nihon Shimbun Kyokai, 2010). Older people typically agree that television, in comparison with all other media forms, features the most interesting advertisements. Television advertising is the most trusted advertising form for older women and the second most trusted (after newspapers) for older men (Nikkei Kokoku Kenkyujo, 2009). In short, television and the associated advertisements play a major role in the life of the Japanese, especially older people. Taken together, these factors can increase our understanding of how television advertisements shape the audience's perception of social groups, which will be discussed in greater detail in the following section.

Media effects on (consumer) socialization

Several theories help us to understand the possible effects of the media and advertising on (consumer) socialization. Two theories that are especially helpful for understanding the possible effects of advertising are social cognitive theory and cultivation theory. *Social cognitive theory* (Bandura, 2009) claims that learning about the social environment can occur through direct or vicarious observations (such as watching television). People model their behavior based on these observations, for example, appropriate age roles. Thus, both younger and older people may learn about appropriate behavior and roles for their respective age groups through advertising and the media. *Cultivation theory* (Gerbner, 1998; Morgan et al., 2009) argues that television has an even stronger influence. Television, a major storyteller of our time, plays an important role in creating often distorted views of reality, especially for heavy viewers. Watching television produces a worldview for the viewers' images of social behavior, norms, and values that are consistent with those provided on television. In short, those who watch a lot of television may believe that older people are only a small proportion of the entire population because they rarely are seen on television, or they may obtain negative feelings about older people because of negative stereotypes portrayed in the media.

Both of these theories emphasize the social influence of media images. Research has confirmed that both theories are accurate in that the media has an influence on how older people regard themselves, how satisfied they are with their lives (Donlon, Ashman, & Levy, 2005; Korzenny & Neuendorf, 1980; Mares & Cantor, 1992; Rahtz, Sirgy, & Meadow, 1988), and how they are regarded by younger people (Gerbner, Gross, Signorielli, & Morgan, 1980; Passuth & Cook, 1985). In addition, research has shown that self-stereotyping of older people and a negative self-image can even lead to negative physiological effects, such as impaired memory performance and hearing decline (Levy, Slade, & Gill, 2006; Westerhof, Harink, Van Selm, Strick, & Van Baaren, 2010).

Television also plays a role in consumer socialization (O'Guinn & Shrum, 1997; Rahtz, Sirgy, & Meadow, 1989; Shrum, Burroughs,

& Rindfleisch, 2005; Shrum et al., 1998). In a longitudinal study of television advertising effects, Moschis and Moore's (1982) data suggested that television advertising may have both short-term and long-term effects on consumer socialization, depending upon a number of mediating variables, such as family communication about consumption. Despite the fact that older consumers mostly reject the notion that they are influenced by television advertising (R. H. Davis & Westbrook, 1985), other evidence suggests that advertising in the media, and television especially, can play a part in shaping older consumers' product preferences (Smith et al., 1985). Gunter (1998) concurs by stating, "Mass media may have an important role in consumer socialization which stretches far beyond children and teenagers, to influence the consumer behaviour patterns of older adults as well" (p. 113).

Indeed, mass media has been identified as one of the most influential sources of consumer socialization in later life (Moschis, 1987; Moschis, Mathur, & Smith, 1993; Smith & Moschis, 1985), and empirical evidence indicates that aging and exposure to advertising may affect several aspects of the consumer behavior of older people, including the rejection of negative or non-desirable portrayal of older people in advertising (Smith, Moschis, & Moore, 1984; Smith et al., 1985). Research has shown that the way in which older television viewers feel represented by a company in its advertisements has an influence on the overall company image and purchase intentions (Festervand & Lumpkin, 1985; Kohlbacher, Prieler et al., 2011a; Kolbe & Burnett, 1992; T. Robinson, Popovich, Gustafson, & Fraser, 2003). Additionally, there are potential negative effects of consumers' comparisons with models in advertisements (Richins, 1991), and advertisements, which consumers find congruent with their self-concept, are more effective in terms of brand preference and purchase intention (Hoffmann, Liebermann, & Schwarz, 2012; Hong & Zinkhan, 1995). Indeed, this so-called self-congruity effect between brand personalities and targeted consumers' self-concepts has been shown to be rather strong and robust (Aguirre-Rodriguez, Bosnjak, & Sirgy, 2012). Therefore, one important consideration is how and with which models older people are addressed. Note that this may also have implications for corporate social responsibility in terms of the portrayal of these models or spokespersons (Carrigan & Szmigin, 2000b; Peterson & Ross, 1997). Overall, this section has shown that the media has effects on (consumer) socialization and attitudes toward older people; this will be the focus of the final section of this chapter.

Attitudes toward older people

What it means to be an older person is socially constructed and thus varies by culture and society (Fung, 2013). Despite cultural differences, in most cultures attitudes toward older people are more negative than toward younger people (Bai, 2014; Kite & Johnson, 1988). For example, Hummert (1990) found that negative stereotypes are thought to be more characteristic of older people and positive stereotypes more for younger people. Similarly, Cuddy and associates (2005) found older people to be regarded as warm and incompetent across several cultures. Perceptions and images of age and older people are strongly influenced by several factors, one of which is the knowledge about and contact with older people. People who have more frequent contact with older people were found to have more positive perceptions of them (Bai, 2014). Thus, the media could play an important role, especially for people who are not frequently meeting older people, in showing more realistic and diverse images of this age group.

In contrast to mostly negative perceptions of older people in the West, Western scholars have frequently stressed the Japanese respect for older people (e.g., Palmore & Maeda, 1985). Honorific language and priority in seating for older people might have been reasons for this conclusion (Koyano, 1989) which is derived from the Confucian tradition that evokes a stronger respect toward older people (O'Leary, 1993). However, several studies have found strong negative attitudes toward older people by the Japanese (Koyano, 1989). This is especially prevalent in the case of older women (Formanek, 2008). O'Leary (1993) shows in an overview of past studies on attitudes toward older people in Japan that there are many more negative stereotypes associated with older people than positive stereotypes. Negative stereotypes include "behind the times," "stubborn," "grumpy," "loss of health," "lonely," and "weak," while positive images include "experienced," "kind," "warm," and "trustworthy" (O'Leary, 1993).

Younger as well as older people in Japan have less favorable images of older people than their counterparts in China and the United States (Levy, 1999). Similarly, Huang (2013) found that attitudes toward aging are more positive in Western than in Eastern countries which might be connected with a weakening of the traditional respect for older people in Eastern countries. Harwood and associates (1996) found little evidence to support the idea of positive evaluations of older people in Asian cultures. Similarly, Bai (2014) summarized his literature review by stating that a positive bias toward older people in East Asia is absent in most studies.

So, how can this seeming contradiction be explained when, on the one hand, Japanese culture traditionally respects older people, but on the other hand there are more negative attitudes toward older people in Japan than in other countries? Soeda (1978) and later Koyano (1989) explain this seemingly contradictory behavior with the Japanese concepts of *tatemae* and *honne*. *Tatemae* is the behavior shown in public, which is culturally accepted and expected based on position or circumstance, while *honne* is a person's true feelings. In other words, Koyano (1989) argues that respect for older people is only *tatemae* and is only a custom without substance while the *honne* of the Japanese is their negative attitudes toward older people.

In addition, such contradictions might be connected with attitudes in the past versus those in the present. Tsuji (1997) points out that it is not that simple to say whether attitudes toward older people and the lives of older people in Japan have become more positive or negative. On the one hand, demographic change creates numerous new problems connected with and for older people, but, on the other hand, older people can also choose their own lifestyle and alternative ways of aging. The future is likely to look different again as outlined in the section on demographic change.

This chapter gave an overview of the aging society and its effects on advertising. In addition, it explained the information sources of older people and their possible effects on the attitudes toward them, and thus sets the stage for the following chapters.

2
Characteristics of Japanese Television Advertising

This chapter will give a short introduction to Japanese advertising (including advertising agencies, advertising media, and television advertisements) and then introduces some of the so-called specialties of Japanese television advertising and offer common explanations and discussion of these characteristics. We will conclude, however, that most of these "specialties" are actually myths and are not unique to Japan and lack empirical evidence. As noted by previous researchers, many accounts are based only on personal observations, rather than empirical data (McCreery, 2000; Moeran, 1996; Praet, 1999). In short, this chapter will debunk the myths about Japanese advertising and show that cultural explanations are not sufficient, in and of themselves; it is necessary to take factors other than culture into account. For example, considering these so-called specialties in an international context will show whether they are really unique to Japan, as claimed by several articles, or whether they might be based either on the sole referent system of the United States or some form of exoticization by foreigners and/or self-exoticization by the Japanese (see also Prieler, 2008b).

Introduction to Japanese advertising

Japan has the third-largest advertising industry in the world (WARC, 2014), but its advertising industry and advertisements are relatively unknown in the West. There have been numerous articles on Japanese advertising during and after Japan's economic boom in the 1980s (for a summary see Praet, 1999), but this area has received comparatively little attention since the turn of the century (Cheng & Kim, 2010), except for some articles by Okazaki and associates (Okazaki & Mueller, 2008, 2011; Okazaki, Mueller, & Taylor, 2010) focusing on the globalization and development of Japanese advertising practices.

Japanese advertising agencies

Dentsu is one of the biggest advertising agencies in the world (see Table 2.1) and the biggest player in advertising in Japan. Together with Hakuhodo and Asatsu-DK, Dentsu dominates the advertising market. For companies that want to advertise in expensive mediums, such as television, it is nearly impossible to ignore these big players. Advertising agencies have to buy time blocks in advance, so it is no wonder that, especially for advertisements aired during prime-time programs, only the "big players" can afford such investments, leading to an oligopoly in this area.

Dentsu's position must also be understood through its history of not only having produced the first advertisement for Japanese television in 1953, but also of having strongly supported the

Table 2.1 The world's top agency companies in 2013 (adapted from Nikkei Kokoku Kenkyujo, 2014)

Rank in 2013	Advertising/Marketing Organizations	Main Branch	Billings in 2013 (in billions of US dollars)
1	WPP	London	17.252
2	Omnicom Group	New York	14.585
3	Publicis Group	Paris	9.232
4	Interpublic Group of Cos.	New York	7.122
5	Dentsu Inc.	Tokyo	5.782
6	Havas	Puteaux, France	2.353
7	Hakuhodo DY Holdings	Tokyo	1.841
8	Alliance Data Systems Corp's Epsilon	Irving, Texas	1.380
9	IBM Corp's IBM Interactive Experience	Armonk, N.Y.	1.250
10	MDC Partners	New York	1.149
20	Asatsu-DK	Tokyo	0.466

television industry, which led to dependencies on both sides. Due to its importance, Dentsu even influences programming, not only indirectly by providing advertisements, but also (as with other big advertising companies) by creating new program ideas for television stations. This is typical for advertising agencies in Japan. For example, another advertising agency, Asatsu-DK, is a famous anime producer that provides TV channels with anime and advertisements (Moeran, 1996).

Among its many activities, Dentsu also founded The Yoshida Hideo Memorial Foundation in 1965, a nonprofit organization, named after Yoshida Hideo, the fourth president of the company, which is promoting advertising research to make a contribution to Japan's economical, industrial, and cultural advancement. In order to realize its goals, the Foundation's activities include establishing grants for researchers in marketing and advertising fields, commissioning research by outside academic groups, publishing *Ad Studies* (a quarterly bulletin), and managing the Advertising Museum Tokyo. The Foundation also supported the research project leading to this book (see www.yhmf.jp).

One specialty of Japanese advertising agencies is "account splitting," which is when an agency deals with the accounts of two competing companies. For example, the same advertising agency may deal with advertising for both Nissan and Toyota. Although separate teams deal with these accounts, they are nonetheless part of the same company. On the other hand, Japanese companies often engage different advertising agencies for different media or give different products to different advertising agencies during the course of individual advertising campaigns. One reason that single agencies take on competing accounts might be simply that the advertising industry is highly concentrated, with only a few big players. This practice may have implications for Japanese advertising, as we will show in a following section.

Advertising media

Within all the advertising media in Japan the strongest segment is promotional media, which include items such as bulk mail, newspaper inserts, and advertising in or on public transportation (Table 2.2). However, within the mass media television advertising is clearly dominant, and is also the single most dominant medium

Table 2.2   Advertising expenditure by media in 2014 (adapted from Dentsu, 2015)

Media	Ratio of Advertising Expenditure
Television	31.8%
Newspapers	9.8%
Magazines	4.1%
Radio	2.1%
Internet	17.1%
Promotional Media	35.1%

overall, since promotional advertisements include several types of advertisements.

The choice of an advertising medium is highly connected to the characteristics of the medium being considered and to what degree it is useful for advertising the product in a given environment. Naturally, there is a difference between print and radio advertisements, which use unisensory ways of communicating, and television, which relies on multisensory methods of transporting meaning and extending its reach. Therefore, the products most advertised on television in Japan are ones whose visibility is important: namely, toiletries, cosmetics, food, and drinks (Nikkei Kokoku Kenkyujo, 2014).

However, television also has its drawbacks. More information, for example, can be entered into print than television advertisements. As a result, print advertisements are perceived as more informative than television advertisements (Nihon Shimbun Kyokai, 2010). Thus, television is frequently used to enhance consumer knowledge of product names, but it is not so favored for communicating information (Moeran, 1996). Moreover, television is the most expensive form of advertising and cannot perfectly address targeted groups, as can specialized magazines.

Before going into detail about Japanese television advertising, and to better understand this at a later point, we will give a short overview of Japanese television.

Japanese television

Japanese television channels can be divided into commercial and non-commercial stations. NHK (*Nippon Hōsō Kyōkai*, Japan

Broadcasting Corporation) is subject to public law and is directly controlled by parliament, so it is dependent on the government, which may lead to a form of self-censorship. NHK is especially known for its programs on information, culture, and education. Programs on NHK do not broadcast television advertisements at this time (as of June 2015).

There are five main commercial television stations in Tokyo that broadcast nearly all over Japan and, unlike NHK, use television advertisements. These stations have some commonalities. Namely, they were all established shortly after NHK, in the 1950s; they are all parts of media groups, mostly in connection with one of Japan's biggest newspapers; and their networks have several stations, all around Japan, that take around 75% of their programming from the main station in Tokyo. Similarly, most television advertisements are broadcast nationwide, but affiliated stations are responsible for organizing some advertisements by themselves, since companies can decide between four types of broadcasting television advertisements. One of these is nationwide broadcasting, while another is local broadcasting. There are also mixed forms, including broadcasting limited to certain areas (Nishimasa, 2006). Hence, companies can choose whether they want to advertise to a station's entire network or just in some areas – for example, in the Tokyo or Osaka regions.

The main commercial television stations are Fuji TV, TBS (*Tōkyō Hōsō*, Tokyo Broadcasting), NTV (*Nihon Terebi*, Nihon Television), TV Asahi, and Tokyo TV. In 2013, Fuji Television clearly attracted the most television advertisements (Table 2.3).

Japanese television advertising

The most expensive time slot for television advertisements is *golden time*, which is called Time A (19.00–22.00). Time Special

Table 2.3 Annual advertising sales, by channel, in 2013 (adapted from Nikkei Kokoku Kenkyujo, 2014)

Television Channel	Sales (in billions of Japanese yen)
Fuji TV	642.145
TBS	354.338
NTV	341.720
TV Asahi	267.928
Tokyo TV	281.500

B encompasses the next-highest peak viewing hours, which are during weekdays (12.00–14.00, 18.00–19.00, and 22.00–23.00) and longer periods during the weekends. Time B is less popular (7.00–10.00 and 14.00–18.00) and is followed by Time C, when almost no one is watching (5.00–7.00, 10.00–12.00, and after 0.00) (Moeran, 1996).

There are two main types of television advertisements on Japanese television. One is spot commercials (*supotto CM*), and the other is program sponsoring or program commercials (*bangumi CM*). A spot commercial is common in most countries around the world and refers to a television advertisement that comes on between two programs and is featured along with spots for other companies. It is different from program commercials in which one program is financed by one or more companies and these companies buy all the rights for advertising breaks during the program's broadcast. In addition, sponsors' advertisements are shown at the beginning, middle, and end of the program, and the main sponsors' names are announced. Spot commercials are clearly more frequent (79.0%) than program commercials (21.0%) (based on Nikkei Kokoku Kenkyujo, 2010).

As discussed later in this chapter in more detail, the most common length of television advertisements is 15 seconds (81.9% of TV advertisements), followed by 30 seconds (15.7%). However, these percentages vary greatly, depending on whether the advertisement is a spot commercial or a program commercial. Most program commercials (51.1%) are 15 seconds, and 44.6% are 30 seconds, while 90.1% of spot commercials are 15 seconds, and only 8.1% are 30 seconds (based on Nikkei Kokoku Kenkyujo, 2010). This finding is not surprising since companies pay for whole advertising breaks during programs in the case of program commercials, so the length of their advertisements makes no actual difference to them, while in the case of spot commercials it is cheaper to use shorter advertisements.

Specialties of Japanese television advertising

In the following we will discuss the most frequent specialties of Japanese television advertisements as mentioned in the literature. These include: (1) atmospheric/mood/soft-sell advertisements; (2) 15-second advertisements; (3) lack of comparative advertising; (4) advertisements with tarento/celebrities; and (5) advertisements with foreigners.

Atmospheric/mood/soft-sell advertisements

The terms "atmospheric ads," "mood ads," and "soft-sell" are often used in the context of Japanese advertising. It is said that Japanese people prefer emotional to informative advertisements. At a time when the standardization discussion of advertising was en vogue, this idea led to many content analyses of the question of hard- versus soft-selling, with advertising from Japan mostly on the soft-sell side (Lin & Salwen, 1995; Mueller, 1987, 1991, 1992; Ramaprasad & Hasegawa, 1992).

Soft-sell advertisements do not show the characteristics of products or companies; instead, using music, colors, symbols, aesthetics, art, and the beauty of nature, among other things, they build emotion and atmosphere that create positive feelings in consumers and, thus, positive associations with products or companies. Since there is often no real message, interpretation of the advertisement's meaning is the viewer's job. The aim is to establish a positive feeling or atmosphere, rather than give consumers reasons to purchase a product (Mooney, 2000). That is why this style of advertising is often referred to as "atmospheric" or "soft-selling," while hard-selling features logical arguments and product information aimed at convincing consumers to buy a product. Praet (1999) summarizes the differences between the approaches taken in Japan and the United States in the following way: "Whereas Western (=US) advertising usually stresses the attributes and function of the product in a rational, direct, and logical way, Japanese advertising generally uses suggestive and indirect appeals" (p. 153). Japanese advertising, for example, uses fewer superlatives, imperatives, and price tags (Belk & Bryce, 1986; Nakanishi, 2002), since the Japanese find such tactics pushy and disturbing (Nakanishi, 2002). As Johannson (1994) observed, Japanese are resistant to hard-selling.

Lin (1993) also found softer sell in Japan with shorter messages, songs, more celebrities, female voices, while US advertisements are more hard-sell with longer messages, male spokespersons, fewer male celebrities, and direct messages. She summarizes that the United States is a "low-context-culture," whereas Japan is a "high-context-culture." In high-context cultures meaning is presumed to derive from individual beliefs, values, norms, and social practices; very little is provided in the coded, explicit, or transmitted portions of messages (see Hall, 1976). Other studies have confirmed such findings

(Keown, Jacobs, Schmidt, & Ghymn, 1992), but have also shown that in South Korea and China even less information is provided in advertisements. In contrast to Lin's findings, Ramaprasad and Hasegawa (1992) have found that Japanese advertisements have more informational content than US advertisements, but they also contain more emotional elements. However, Ramaprasad and Hasegawa (1992) conclude that the informative and emotional strategies in both countries are similar and that very few advertisements have no information at all.

More specific cultural reasons related to Japan are often given for the differing use of atmospheric advertisements in the United States and Japan. Yamada (1997) argues that this issue is connected to the directness of the English language and the indirectness of Japanese. DiBenedetto and associates (1992) also emphasize a more indirect than direct form of expression in the messages in Japanese advertisements. In an interview, Johanna Metzger, from the advertising agency Leo Burnett (Japan), has also explained the phenomenon of soft-selling and mood advertisements in Japan in connection to the directness of English and the indirectness of Japanese (Schlaile, 2000). Schlaile concludes that one characteristic of Japanese society is the large role of non-verbal communication. She underscores this with a statement from Fukuda Toshihiko of the advertising agency Dentsu: "We are very weak in communication" (Schlaile, 2000, p. 8). However, many Japanese advertising executives may be interested in playing with the myth of Japanese uniqueness (Moeran, 1996) and so make themselves irreplaceable.

Moeran (1996) is a harsh critic of such cultural explanations for atmospheric advertisements which often go far beyond referring to the Japanese language and are often based on so-called "unique" Japanese concepts. Moeran argues that many Western writers regard Japanese advertisements as more intuitive or atmospheric and combine this argument with orientalist arguments about Japanese culture. He states that such assertions are never based on data, but on writers' intuitive perceptions which ignore many important issues.

Although Japanese culture can certainly not be ignored when analyzing Japanese advertising, we will outline in the following several points which are often ignored in linear explanations of this phenomenon and show that explanations beyond culture are important for understanding Japanese advertising:

(a) *Research bias toward the United States.* Most comparative studies conclude that Japanese advertisements are unique by comparing them to US advertisements. However, trends similar to those observed in Japan can also be found in other countries. For example, Schmidt and Spiess's (1994) description of German lifestyle advertisements during the 1980s could easily also be used for atmospheric advertisements in Japan. Schmidt and Spiess find that these advertisements use strong images and sound, have almost no story, and feature interchangeable people and scenery whose mood becomes one with the product. French advertisements, which have low informational content, are also very similar to Japanese advertisements in that respect (Zandpour, Chang, & Catalano, 1992).

(b) *Personal observations, rather than empirical data.* As Moeran (1996) rightly stated, many descriptions of Japanese advertisements are based on personal observations rather than empirical data. A large number seem to be based on award-winning Japanese advertisements or prime-time advertisements, while advertisements in the afternoon are largely ignored. In this context, it should also be mentioned that during the last few years there has been a marked increase in infomercials, which are the purest form of hard-sell advertisements, giving the most information. This trend stands in stark contrast to the notion that Japan is a country of soft-sell advertisements.

(c) *Advertising style is connected with economic stage.* A country's advertising style may be also connected to its economic stage. Tse, Belk & Zhou (1989) have shown that the informational content of Chinese advertisements is relatively high, and emotional advertisements are seldom used, whereas in Hong Kong informational content is very low. Taiwan is in the middle of these two countries' results. Based on their findings in these three areas within Chinese culture, it seems there is no real cultural explanation for the informational content of advertisements, though there is an economic one. Holden (2002) also refers, in a comparison of Japanese and Malaysian television advertisements, to the connection between different advertising formats and the economic and political stages of societies. The connection between "economic stages" and advertising style can also be seen in Japanese history. In the 1950s, products, their characteristics, and informational content were the feature of Japanese advertisements. Product details were communicated clearly (Namba, 2002). This remained the case until the end of the 1970s, but at the beginning of the 1980s, mood or atmospheric advertising gradually became predominant (Görtzen, 1995). In short, the move away from mostly information-centered advertisements has occurred since the 1970s (Namba, 2002). However, as interviews with ad executives have shown, Japanese advertisements became more direct again, a shift from emotions to sales, during the economic recession of the 1990s (Okazaki & Mueller, 2011).

(d) *Advertising is not ahistorical.* As the previous point has shown, advertising does not stay the same. Soft-sell and mood advertisements may have been typical during the 1980s, but nowadays the importance of such advertisements is highly overstated. Such overstatements seem to be a reproduction of older ideas. Since the bursting of the economic bubble, advertisements have returned to providing product information, as well as a "slice of life," or scenes from everyday life, with many of the artistic products prevalent in the 1980s disappearing (Haehling von Lanzenauer, 1999). Kawashima (2006) also states that some distinctive features of Japanese advertising, like soft-selling, "indirect forms of expressions, brief dialogue or narration in television advertisements with minimal explanatory content or a (Japanese) sense of humour to create a bond of mutual feelings seem to have gone" (p. 396). He explains this is because "media buying power, rather than creativity, dictates the trade" (Kawashima, 2006, p. 400). Namba (2002) writes that already in the 1990s the trend of atmospheric advertisements had ended and was followed by serialized advertisements. Such changes can also be seen in recent research. Hagiwara and associates (2009) have found a higher percentage of hard-sell advertisements (24.5% in 1997; 26.9% in 2007) than soft-sell advertisements (2.9% in 1997; 5.7% in 2007) in Japan. However, most advertisements were not clearly classifiable as one type or another (72.6% in 1997; 67.4% in 2007). That advertising is steadily changing is shown very well in a study that compared print advertisements from 1978 and 2005 (Okazaki & Mueller, 2008) in which the authors found that Japanese advertisements have become more direct and persuasive, while US advertisements have become more benefit-oriented, with a softer touch. In the United States the prevalence of soft-sell advertisements has increased from 5.2% to 40.8% within all advertisements. Similarly, these researchers (Okazaki et al., 2010) found in another study that soft-sell (but partly also hard-sell) appeals are perceived similarly across the United States and Japan in terms of believability, the degree to which they are irritating, and the attitude toward the advertisement.

(e) *Advertising style depends on advertising media.* Whether an ad is atmospheric or informative depends on the type of media used. Whereas television advertisements tend to be atmospheric, print advertisements tend to be informative (Keown et al., 1992; Moeran, 1996). Generalizations of Japanese advertisements as soft-sell seem to have been weakened in light of studies on print advertisements that show that Japanese advertisements are more informative than their counterparts from the United States (Hong, Muderrisoglu, & Zinkhan, 1987; Madden, Caballero, & Matsukubo, 1986).

(f) *Advertising style depends on product category.* The advertising style and information provided depend highly on the type of product advertised (Ramaprasad & Hasegawa, 1992). Praet (1999) states that advertisements for convenience goods tend to have less information than advertisements for shopping goods since there is lower perceived risk associated with purchasing the former than the latter. Johansson gives another explanation, which is partly cultural, arguing that a more attribute-oriented style is used for products when group conformity is less important. In addition, Johansson (1994) asserts that products that become more similar to other products should be advertised with soft-sell approaches to add value and image to their brands. It should also not be forgotten that atmospheric advertisements are used when consumers already know about the qualities and characteristics of products (Dallmann, 1998), which brings us to the next point.

(g) *Information is provided by other sources.* Advertising in Japan might not have to give much information, since people also get information from sources such as magazines, brochures, and, especially, retail stores. Japan has only half the population of the United States and the land area of California, but it has the same number of retail outlets where consumers can find all kinds of product information (Mooney, 2000). Johansson (1994) notes that real product education in Japan occurs only in stores.

(h) *Audience motivation to process information.* The elaboration likelihood model shows the route by which advertisements persuade consumers. This route depends on how much consumers think about an ad's message. If a consumer is unmotivated to process information, a soft-sell might be best (Cacioppo & Petty, 1985). This may, especially, be the case in Japan where people work long hours daily and only want to be entertained at night. Mooney (2000), as well as Johansson (1994), state that the home is sacred territory, and advertisers need to justify interrupting their programs. A hard-sell approach may be the wrong way to do that.

As can be seen in the previous paragraphs, cultural explanations of the distinguishing characteristics of Japanese advertisements are too simplistic. The same is true of explanations of the prevalence of 15-second advertisements which are also often explained in terms of the Japanese mentality.

15-second advertisements

One of the most often-cited phenomena of Japanese advertisements is their length, which is typically 15 seconds. In many European countries, and in the United States, the average advertisement length is approximately 30 seconds (Yamaki, 1994a). In Japan, 30-second versions of most advertisements exist, but they are rather scantly broadcast in comparison to 15-second versions. Johannson (1994) – referring to data from the advertising agency Grey-Daiko – states that 35% of advertisements in the United States are 15 seconds, while this is the case for 79% of advertisements in Japan. Other studies also indicate a relatively higher amount of short advertisements in Japan – for example 64% in Japan versus 32% in the United States (Ramaprasad & Hasegawa, 1992) and 55.7% in 1997 and 54.7% in 2007 (Hagiwara et al., 2009). Data on television advertisements broadcast in the Kanto region (Greater Tokyo Area) shows that 81.9% of all television advertisements are 15 seconds, while 15.7% are 30 seconds, and 2.4% are of other lengths (based on Nikkei Kokoku Kenkyujo, 2010).

Why do 15-second advertisements predominate? Many Japan experts and advertising executives explain the brevity of these advertisements in terms similar to those used to explain the usage of soft-selling, connecting it to Japan's being a high-context culture and to Japanese fondness for short forms, like haiku (a very short form of Japanese poetry). It is said that the Japanese understand one another without many words or much explanation (for a discussion, see Mooney, 2000). This self-stereotype is often-cited by the Japanese. However, Japan is not the only country in the world with short advertisements. France, which definitely has a cultural background very different from Japan's, is another example (Dallmann, 1998), and we should thus consider other factors that might be at play.

Although it is certainly not possible to entirely answer the question of why 15-second advertisements are frequently used in Japan, economic reasons should be considered. Mooney (2000) refers to the high cost of airing television advertisements and also to the intense competition for airtime. Fifteen-second advertisements began in Japan in 1961, when television stations started selling advertising airtime in 15-second, instead of 30-second, units. This new system totally changed the style of Japanese advertisements (Kawashima, 2006). Though it is unclear what the reasons for that change were, it might have simply been a way of increasing television station revenue in a time shortly after all of Japan's current television stations started broadcasting and at a moment when a lot of new investment in airtime was necessary. Since 30-second spots had been normal in Japan prior to 1961, one has to question whether cultural explanations of 15-second spots suffice. There might be some cultural reasons for the use of shorter advertisements in Japan, but, on the whole, it seems that economic reasons should not be overlooked. In addition, the often-stated difference between the length of advertisements in Japan and the United States, which only started airing 15-second advertisements in the 1980s (Singh & Cole, 1993), seems to be disappearing (Okazaki & Mueller, 2011).

Lack of comparative advertising

Another often-cited phenomenon when comparing Japanese and US advertising is the fact that comparative advertising amounts to approximately 35% of advertising in the United States (Yamaki,

1994b) but barely exists in Japan. Comparative advertising directly or indirectly compares two products (sometimes mentioning names). Empirical research has found less comparison in Japanese advertisements than in US advertisements (Belk & Bryce, 1986; Lin, 1993; Ramaprasad & Hasegawa, 1992). For example, Ramaprasad and Hasegawa (1992) found that 22% are comparative in the United States, while only 10% in Japan.

Comparative advertising has been allowed in Japan since the Japan Fair Trade Commission (FTC) lifted a ban on it in 1987 (Mooney, 2000). However, there are some guidelines, including a prohibition on lying and slandering competitors and a mandate that advertisements include interesting information for consumers (Haehling von Lanzenauer, 1999).

Why comparative advertisements are not used in Japan is often explained culturally. It is said that it is against the Japanese way of thinking to show one's advantages while showing the disadvantages of others. It is impolite to compare products and speak about one's own product too directly and too well. This kind of advertising is said to go against the modest nature of the Japanese who tend to avoid conflict and highly value harmony (Nakanishi, 2002; Praet, 1999). It is important that nobody lose face in Japan (Mooney, 2000). These explanations are focused on the traditional values of what Hofstede (2001) calls "collectivistic" societies which contrast with individualistic societies like the United States.

Nevertheless, there are cases of comparative advertising in Japan. Although direct product comparisons are rare on Japanese television, there are more subtle forms, such as comparisons with other, unnamed products. Nakanishi (2002) gives the example of an ad in which pilots sit in a train and say that it is safer to take the train than fly and is just as fast. Sometimes companies also compare products with their own previous products or against products from foreign companies (Mooney, 2000).

There have also been a few cases of direct comparative advertisements in Japan. The most controversial example was an ad for Pepsi, broadcast in 1991. The advertisement featured the rap singer MC Hammer becoming a crooner after drinking Coca-Cola and becoming a rap singer again after drinking Pepsi. Coca-Cola complained to the Fair Trade Commission, but the Fair Trade Commission said nothing against the advertisement. Nonetheless, television companies quit broadcasting the advertisement, probably because Coca-Cola is a huge advertiser in Japan. Finally, Pepsi made a new version of the advertisement that covered the Coca-Cola bottle and was then broadcast on television. Since everybody was already familiar with the previous contents of the advertisement, this version also led to controversy. Thus it is no wonder that, having experienced a preview of the problems associated with comparative advertising, television stations have shown little interest in it (Mooney, 2000).

The few examples of comparative advertising that exist, however, have not clearly proven that Japanese people are discouraged from buying products by such advertisements (Mooney, 2000). Yamaki (1994b) stresses that there are non-cultural reasons for the scarcity of these types of advertisements, including business and economic concerns. One such concern is the previously mentioned presence of competing accounts at many advertising agencies (i.e., account splitting) which sometimes deal with the accounts of competing companies. If an advertising agency makes comparative advertisements for companies for whom they are in charge, they may have trouble with one of those companies.

In conclusion, there are almost no direct forms of product comparison on Japanese television, as there are in the United States, at this time. Nevertheless, the degree to which this has to do with Japanese culture must be questioned. There is certainly a connection between culture and advertisements, but in many other countries without the so-called "Japanese mentality," and also in many other individualistic societies, direct comparisons of products are not used. One might ask whether the question is the wrong one and whether research should focus on why comparative advertising exists in the United States (Beard, 2013) and not in Japan and many other countries – rather than concentrating on why it does not exist in Japan.

Advertisements with tarento/celebrities

Tarento comes from the English word "talent" and means "a major media personality." Tarento are omnipresent on Japanese television and in Japanese advertisements (see also Prieler, Kohlbacher, Hagiwara, & Arima, 2010). They appear in talk shows, quiz shows, advertisements, and variety shows. Previous research has found that the percentage of advertisements featuring celebrities varies from approximately 50% (W.-N. Lee, Choi, & Tsai, 2007; Praet, 2009) to

70% (Hagiwara et al., 2009; Mooney, 2000). This phenomenon plays also a role for older celebrities (Prieler et al., 2010), as will be shown in Chapter 3.

Celebrities are considered one of the best ways to attract attention to a company's products in an age of communication clutter (Moeran, 1996; Okazaki & Mueller, 2011), and they help products stand out from the competition (Mooney, 2000). Moeran (1996) also suggests that celebrities are used to create product image. This is similar to what McCracken (1989) has shown with the meaning-transfer model where a celebrity's significance is transferred to the products he or she endorses. This works especially well when a "match-up" between product and celebrity exists (Kamins, 1990).

Praet (2001) details additional reasons for celebrity sponsorship: celebrities are often used as a shared vocabulary between agency and client, since celebrities are easier to discuss than complicated advertising concepts. Celebrities are also used as a form of risk avoidance and to replace the product concept. In other words, celebrities have proven effective in Japan, and, since they already carry meaning, this makes actual product concepts less important. Some scholars have criticized the extreme concentration on celebrities at the expense of other concepts (e.g., Kawashima, 2006). They have argued that advertisers do not want to take any risks and so concentrate on celebrities, rather than big ideas, thereby leading to lower-quality advertisements.

Celebrities, however, do not only confer advantages in advertising. They pose risks as well. They may overshadow brands (in other words, the celebrity is remembered, but not the product). They may also be overexposed (used to sell too many different products) or simply be too expensive (Erdogan, 1999). Finally, negative events connected with celebrities may damage the brands they represent. In fact, a meta-analysis of 32 articles on celebrities showed that negative information about celebrities had a larger impact on the effects of endorsement than did any positive endorsement strategy (Amos, Holmes, & Strutton, 2008).

Since the advantages and disadvantages of using celebrities to sell products hold true in many countries, it is worth asking what makes the Japanese case so different that celebrities are used so comparatively often. Celebrities play very different roles in the Japanese media than they do in the media of other countries and cannot be compared directly to Western celebrities. While many Western celebrities seem hard to approach, untouchable, and almost otherworldly, Japanese celebrities are more like everyday people, like neighbors. In accordance with this image they are shown in everyday situations in advertisements (Mooney, 2000; Painter, 1996). In Japanese culture it is very bad manners to show off and put oneself at the center of events; modesty, regardless of social status, is part of Japan's culture of politeness (Davies & Ikeno, 2002). This social code also seems to apply to celebrities.

The phenomenon of celebrity in Japan must also be seen in the wider context of the Japanese media, where they are omnipresent. Indeed, almost every television program in Japan features multiple celebrities. They act in dramas, sing, and appear on television variety and quiz shows, as well as in the advertisements that run between segments of these shows. Celebrities, in Japanese culture, are almost regarded as part of people's families or peer groups since the average Japanese sees them every day and knows much about their private lives. It is not surprising that celebrities speak to their audiences as if speaking directly to friends (Mooney, 2000). This is a "quasi-intimate interaction" (Painter, 1996), or what some have called a "parasocial interaction" (Horton & Wohl, 1956), where people process mass-mediated communications as they would interpersonal interactions. Audiences follow the details of celebrities' entire lives, often including events in their childhood, adolescence, and marriage, as well as the birth of their children, middle age, and death. Television produces celebrities and keeps them popular by giving them constant exposure, including of their private lives (Painter, 1996).

For young and aspiring actors, appearing in advertisements can be the first step toward a career in television and film. If appearing in an advertisement increases an actor's popularity, this can lead to contracts for television dramas or quiz and variety shows. Some celebrities actually gain fame through advertising (Mooney, 2000; Praet, 2001). Unlike in Hollywood, television advertisements in Japan *can* enhance a film star's career (Nakanishi, 2002) or be an important way for models, singers, and entertainers to increase their popularity (Praet, 2001). Even appearing in several advertisements at the same time is not a problem, as this serves to demonstrate a celebrity's popularity (Mooney, 2000) and is very common in Japan.

The structure of the Japanese media must also be considered when explaining the role of celebrities in advertising. Traditionally, Japanese advertising agencies have maintained very close links to the media and entertainment industries. Advertising agencies often organize big events and concerts and sometimes even develop new program ideas for television channels (Moeran, 1996). Arguably this intermarriage between advertising agencies and the media and entertainment industries has also led to mutual interest in promoting the celebrities they all feature. For example, advertising agencies may use a celebrity who will star in a new drama at the same time as the launch of a product they are promoting (Moeran, 1996). Thus, the advertisement in which the celebrity appears becomes a reminder of the drama, and the drama becomes a reminder of the advertisement (and its product) which will be broadcast during the advertising breaks in the drama. Additionally, a musician might use an advertisement to promote him/herself or a new song.

Japan has one of the highest amounts of celebrity usage in television advertising in the world. As Praet (2009) has shown in comparative research on advertisements in 25 countries, only one other country, South Korea, features a similar number of celebrities in television advertisements. Analyzing the percentage of celebrities in television advertising, Praet finds three groups of countries: one in which 50% or more of advertisements used celebrities, including Japan and Korea; one in which around 25% of advertisements featured celebrities, including Brazil, China, Hong Kong, and Malaysia; and Western countries, where celebrities are not very common in advertisements (less than 15%).

There have been relatively few explanations for the high usage of celebrities in Japan. To better understand this phenomenon, Praet (2009) correlates the number of celebrities in different countries with Hofstede's (2001) dimensions of power distance, uncertainty avoidance, masculinity-femininity, and individualism-collectivism. Only the last "dimension" (individualism-collectivism) reveals significant results, indicating that individualism-collectivism may be a clue as to why celebrities are so dominant in Japanese advertising. At the same time, the use of celebrities to advertise products in a collectivistic culture like Japan might seem like a contradiction at first, since the "cult of personality can be seen as a product of the myth of the individual" (Moeran, 1996, p. 164). However, Japanese celebrities do not develop their public images according to this myth, unlike their Western counterparts, as noted previously. Overall, however, one also has to question whether the popularity of celebrities in advertisements is not an East Asian phenomenon (for example, they are also dominant in South Korea [S. M. Choi, Lee, & Kim, 2005; Praet, 2009]) having more to do with the Asian media industry than with dimensions such as individualism and collectivism which seem to be deteriorating in the age of globalization.

One area of celebrity usage in Japan that is much spoken about is the use of foreign celebrities (for a discussion see Mooney, 2000). Western celebrities who have appeared in Japanese television advertisements include, for example, Charles Bronson, Alain Delon, David Niven, Peter Fonda, Orson Welles, Sophia Loren, John McEnroe, Paul Newman, Placido Domingo, Madonna, Sylvester Stallone, Woody Allen, Pierce Brosnan, Mariah Carey, Leonardo DiCaprio, Celine Dion, Harrison Ford, Jodie Foster, Brad Pitt, Mickey Rourke, Charlie Sheen, Meg Ryan, Bruce Willis, Brooke Shields, and Arnold Schwarzenegger (Fields, 1983; Görtzen, 1995; M. Yamada, 2005).

However, while there is much talk about foreign celebrities in Japan, in reality the frequency of their appearance in television advertisements is relatively low. This might also be attributed to the economic recession of the 1990s (Okazaki & Mueller, 2011), but even before that Mueller (1992) found only 0.9% to be foreign celebrities. Prieler (2006b) found that only 15 of a sample of 3,352 unduplicated television advertisements included Western celebrities. One reason for the impression that Western celebrities have much higher visibility than they actually do may be that the advertisements in which they appear are generally often repeated and talked about. A much more significant number of advertisements, however, feature anonymous foreigners who are the main focus of the next section.

Advertisements with foreigners

Japanese advertisements feature numerous foreign elements, including foreign languages, scenery, music, and artifacts. Except for a few studies focusing on these elements (Hagiwara, 2004; Prieler, 2006a, 2006b; Sherry & Camargo, 1987), the most discussed and most popular research area has been the representation of foreigners, since this is most striking when watching Japanese television advertisements.

The use of foreigners in Japanese television advertisements began in 1961, with the musical group Trio Los Panchos (Creighton, 1994). It grew during the 1970s and, especially, during the 1980s. Since that time the numbers have not changed much. Hagiwara (2004) has found, in a comparative study of advertisements aired between 1993 and 2003, few changes: 18.6% of advertisements included foreigners in 2003, compared to 15.0% in 1993. Hagiwara has also shown that, within some product categories, foreigners dominate. Of advertisements for automobiles, for example, 51.1% include foreigners.

However, who are these foreigners, specifically? Hagiwara (2004) finds a clear predominance of white people (78.0% in 1993, 72.9% in 2003), followed by non-Japanese Asian people (9.3% in 1993, 10.6% in 2003), black people (3.2% in 1993, 3.7% in 2003), and other groups. This finding is in accordance with other studies (Creighton, 1995; Hiyoshi, 2001; Iwao, 1984; Kozakai, 1996; Martin, 2005; Martin & Woodside, 2007; Prieler, 2010).

Prieler (2010) is referring, in this context, to an artificial "racial hierarchy" that is based on a "ladder of civilizations" (Sugimoto, 2010) adopted from the West. He concludes that white people are not only numerically dominant, but are also shown in much more diverse ways and are used to advertise a wider range of products than are people of other races. Black people, in contrast, are shown as musicians or athletes (even celebrities are confined to these roles; for a discussion on black people in Japan, see Russell, 1991), while Asians are shown as celebrities or else associated with products from their countries of origin.

However, this still does not answer the question of why foreigners and foreign elements are actually used in Japanese television advertisements. Prieler (2006b) names two major reasons: (1) to attract attention, and (2) to transfer to a product an image that already is associated with the foreign person, place, language, or music featured. The latter idea is similar to McCracken's meaning-transfer model (McCracken, 1989). Meaning transfers are possible in Japan since ethnocultural stereotypes there are strong – both positive and negative. Haarmann (1984) observes, for example, that the French language stands for high elegance or refined taste. Creighton (1995) notes that Western foreigners are bearers of innovation and style in Japan, and Ramaprasad and Hasegawa (1990) state that "Japanese attach attributes such as value, modernism, and newness with the use of Western symbols" (p. 1030). On a more general level, depictions of foreignness give products a more global look. Since advertisements are mostly only interested in the positive features of the products they sell, cultures with high prestige value are used in television advertisements. This brings our discussion back to Prieler's (2010) "racial hierarchy" in Japan. In Japan, prestige and positive values are mainly associated with the West, which is why other places and people are rarely used in television advertisements. Why these depictions of the foreign are rather limited in Japan is beyond the scope of this chapter (for a discussion, see Prieler, 2010).

Foreigners in Japanese television advertisements definitely have a strong appearance. However, one should also keep in mind that this phenomenon exists in other Asian countries. For example, Prieler (2012b) has shown that a large amount of Korean television advertisements feature foreigners (17.5%), and 80.0% of these foreigners are white people. In short, the numbers in Korea are very similar to the figures in Japan. Similar to Japanese magazine advertisements (Morimoto & Chang, 2009), research on South Korean print advertisements has even shown that white models are more common than Korean models (Nam, Lee, & Hwang, 2011). This finding was also true in a study by Frith, Shaw, and Cheng (2005) who have found an even more pronounced trend toward the use of white people in print advertisements in Singapore and Taiwan where white models are more prevalent than native models.

Conclusion

We hope this chapter helped debunk some of the myths about Japanese television advertising and its so-called "specialties." We do not deny the cultural aspects of Japanese advertisements, as advertisements and media are embedded in the cultures of their countries, but, as Moeran (1996) stated, many interpretations of the defining characteristics of Japanese advertising "smell" of orientalism, or, if produced by the Japanese, a form of self-orientalism. Especially in the case of advertising, there are also factors other than culture at work, including economic imperatives, that should not be ignored. This can be seen in the case of 15-second spots, whose use is partly based on the high cost of airtime in Japan, or the case of atmospheric advertisements which may be connected to some kind of "economic stage," or, finally, to the case of comparative advertising, where advertising companies may get into trouble with their clients if they hold competing accounts.

Many studies of Japanese advertising seem to assume that advertising is non-developing and that its "specialties" are somehow ahistorical, as if Japanese advertising has always been the way it is, which then means that the only way to understand it is through cultural interpretations that delve into Japanese history. However, in reality, Japanese advertising – as every other cultural form – is undergoing continuous change. Much of what is written about Japanese advertising is a reproduction of older works that are based on even older data or no data at all. Another problem is that the so-called "specialties" that distinguish Japanese advertisements are based only on comparisons with the United States that often claim to be comparisons with "Western advertising." Such comparisons are rather one-sided. There is no uniform West, as there is no uniform Asia, and this is true in many respects, including advertising. German advertisements are certainly different from Japanese advertisements, which are also different from Italian advertisements. Also, if compared to the advertising industries of countries other than the United States, Japan's advertising becomes much less special, though some cultural specificity should not be neglected. After all, Europe also has a cultural background quite different from Japan's, so differences should not be surprising. In conclusion, this chapter does not purport to be the last word on Japanese advertising which will assuredly shift again, as it has always done in the past. But it has hopefully set the stage for the following chapters of this book, providing the reader with fundamental background information about advertising and advertisements in Japan.

3
The Representation of Older People in Japanese Television Advertisements

In this chapter we present and discuss research on the representation of older people in Japanese television advertisements based on a content analysis of around 3,000 television advertisements. The chapter is structured as follows: We first discuss the theoretical background of this study. The following section will give an overview of the important literature on the representation of older people in television advertising and introduce the main variables of this research. Then we present the results for each variable. We also compare the results between 1997 and 2007 and thus analyze if there were any changes in how older people were represented in Japanese television advertisements between 1997 and 2007, and if these changes were connected with social changes in Japan. These results will then be further analyzed in the discussion section.

The representation of social groups in advertising has been a major concern in academia. Though several studies have investigated representations of ethnicities and gender in television advertisements (e.g., Furnham & Mak, 1999; Taylor & Stern, 1997), research focusing on older people has been comparatively scant. However, during the previous decades there have been several studies on the representation of older people in the media (Bai, 2014) and specifically in television advertisements (Y. B. Zhang et al., 2006). These studies are predominantly from Anglophone countries such as the United States, Canada, the United Kingdom, and Australia. Only a few English-language studies have also investigated this topic in other countries, such as South Korea (B.-K. Lee, Kim, & Han, 2006;

Ong & Chang, 2009), China (Y. B. Zhang, Song, & Carver, 2008), Malaysia (Ong & Chang, 2009; Sudbury-Riley & Idris, 2013), Germany (Kessler, Schwender, & Bowen, 2010), and our own work on Japan (Hagiwara, Kohlbacher, Prieler, & Arima, 2010; Hagiwara et al., 2009; Prieler, 2008a; Prieler, Kohlbacher, Hagiwara, & Arima, 2009b; Prieler et al., 2010, 2011a; Prieler, Kohlbacher, Hagiwara, & Arima, 2011b; Prieler et al., 2015) on which this chapter is based.

Our research is one of the first longitudinal studies (comparing television advertisements in 1997 and 2007), which gives us the opportunity to investigate whether advertisements reflect social changes and if the representation of older people in Japanese television advertising indicates the rising importance of older people (Harwood & Anderson, 2002). The increasing proportion of older people in many countries makes this issue ever more pressing.

Theoretical framework

There are several theories relevant to research on older people in advertisements. Some scholars argue that advertising reflects social norms (Frith & Mueller, 2010), while others suggest that advertising creates and teaches social roles and values (Pollay, 1986). The former is supported by *ethnolinguistic vitality theory* (Giles, Bourghis, & Taylor, 1977) which addresses the content of advertising and is important for understanding the position of a group within a society (Y. B. Zhang et al., 2006). It evaluates a group's strength in society based on status, demographics, and institutional support, which includes the group's representation in the media. In short, using the media is only one of several ways to evaluate the group's strength. Content analysis of groups in the media indicates the group's value and respect within a society. In other words, frequent and positive representations indicate a group's vitality, strength, and influence in society (Abrams, Eveland, & Giles, 2003; Harwood & Anderson, 2002), while rare and negative representations indicate that the group has little influence in society. Thus, the claim of the ethnolinguistic vitality theory is that one can use media representations to analyze the role and influence a social group has within society.

Another reason for the importance of analyzing advertising content is connected with its possible effects. Though the results of content analysis cannot demonstrate effects on audiences, content analysis is an essential first step in the process of grasping the possible impacts of media influence (Riffe, Lacy, & Fico, 2005). Two theories that are especially helpful for understanding the possible effects of advertising are social cognitive theory and cultivation theory (see Chapter 1). Both theories emphasize the social influence of media images. Research has shown that the media indeed has an influence on how older people regard themselves and how they are regarded by other people (e.g., Donlon et al., 2005; Gerbner et al., 1980; Mares & Cantor, 1992; Passuth & Cook, 1985; see also Chapter 1).

Literature review

The following overview of existing literature helps situate our results in a more global context. However, comparisons between our research and past studies require caution because earlier research was based upon different cultural contexts, sample sizes and sampling methods (prime time vs. whole day, duplicated vs. unduplicated television advertisements), and varying definitions of "older people" (ranging from age 45 or older to age 65 years or older). The variables we have found most important for analyzing representation of older people in television advertisements are derived and adapted from previous research on social groups focusing on the following areas: age groups in television advertisements, frequency of representation of older people (including by gender), perceived importance, celebrity versus non-celebrity, the image of older people, social interaction, setting, and product categories.

Frequency of older people (by gender)

Over- or under-representation of social groups in the media is a possible indicator of their importance, relevance, and recognition within society (Gerbner et al., 1980; Signorielli & Bacue, 1999). It can also affect public knowledge and perceptions of these groups as well as the view that society has of these groups (Abrams et al., 2003). For example, young people may come to believe that the number of older people in the population is small (Gerbner et al., 1980). Many previous studies have found that older people were underrepresented in television advertisements compared to the demographic reality (Bai, 2014; Ylänne, 2015). This was demonstrated in articles published in the United States (Atkins, Jenkins,

& Perkins, 1990/1991; Greco, 1993; Langmeyer, 1993; M. M. Lee, Carpenter, & Meyers, 2007; Peterson & Ross, 1997; Roy & Harwood, 1997). For example, Gerbner and associates (1980) reported that the underrepresentation of people began somewhat under the age of 50 for prime-time advertisements. Langmeyer (1993) reported that 12.3% of television advertisements featured people age 60 or older, although this group constituted 16.7% of the population. Research defining older people as age 45 or older (Peterson & Ross, 1997), age 50 or older (Atkins et al., 1990/1991), and age 55 or older (M. M. Lee et al., 2007) obtained similar results. The underrepresentation of older people has also been found in other parts of the world, such as Australia (Higgs & Milner, 2006), South Korea (B.-K. Lee et al., 2006; Ong & Chang, 2009), and Germany (Kessler et al., 2010). Lee and associates (2006) reported that older people were represented in 8.0% of advertisements although they constituted 12% of the population in South Korea. Ong and Chang (2009) also found the same underrepresentation in South Korea (8.6% vs. 13.3%) and Malaysia (2.5% vs. 6.6%). However, a few studies have reported results that were closer to demographic reality, such as in China (Y. B. Zhang et al., 2008), the United Kingdom (Simcock & Sudbury, 2006), and the United States (B.-K. Lee et al., 2006).

In terms of age distribution within the advertisements by gender, almost all previous studies found that television advertisements featured a higher percentage of older men than women. This finding was true in North America (Atkins et al., 1990/1991; Fullerton & Kendrick, 2000; Ganahl, Prinsen, & Netzley, 2003; Hiemstra, Goodman, Middlemiss, Vosko, & Ziegler, 1983; M. M. Lee et al., 2007; Milner & Collins, 2000; Roy & Harwood, 1997), in Europe (Furnham & Farragher, 2000; Milner & Collins, 2000; Neto & Pinto, 1998; Simcock & Sudbury, 2006; Uray & Burnaz, 2003), in Asia (Furnham, Mak, & Tanidjojo, 2000; B.-K. Lee et al., 2006; Milner & Collins, 2000; Ong & Chang, 2009; Prieler, 2012a; Prieler & Centeno, 2013; Singh & Cole, 1993; Siu & Au, 1997; Sudbury-Riley & Idris, 2013), and in Australia (Gilly, 1988; Milner & Higgs, 2004). The same trend was also reported in a Japanese context (Prieler et al., 2009b, 2011a; Yamanaka, 2000), but exceptions were found in Anglophone countries (Furnham & Bitar, 1993; Furnham & Farragher, 2000; Stern & Mastro, 2004; Swayne & Greco, 1987), and in Spain (Valls-Fernández & Martínez-Vicente, 2007).

Perceived importance and celebrities

It is also necessary to examine the roles older people play in the advertisements (i.e., major, minor, or background roles) because frequency of representations can only provide a limited picture of the perceived importance of older people. The roles that older people play in advertisements may indicate their perceived social value. For example, a major role for an older person could indicate importance. Through watching television, the audience learns what roles are "appropriate" to older people and forms beliefs about these groups (Abrams et al., 2003; Gerbner et al., 1980), thus cultivating an image of what roles older people should play in society. In studies that have investigated the roles played by older people in television advertisements, the overall trend in the United States and the United Kingdom is that an increasing number of older people appear in minor or background roles than in major roles (Bai, 2014; Greco, 1993; Roy & Harwood, 1997; Simcock & Sudbury, 2006). For example, Roy and Harwood (1997) reported 38.2% in major roles, 19.5% in minor roles, and 52.8% in background roles. Greco (1993) found that older people were featured mainly in minor roles (56%) in 1985, followed by major roles (32%), and background roles (12%); similarly, in 1990, 27% of older people were in major roles, 41% in minor, and 32% in background roles. In contrast to these findings, research in South Korea has found that more older people play major roles than minor or background roles (B.-K. Lee et al., 2006; Ong & Chang, 2009). For example, Lee and associates (2006) found that there are more older people in major roles (86.1%) than in minor roles (13.9%), and Ong and Chang (2009) reported that older people were depicted mainly in major roles.

Whether older people in major roles are celebrities or non-celebrities communicates different messages to the audience. As previously mentioned (see Chapter 2), celebrities play an important role in Japanese television advertisements. Studies have reported celebrities appearing in approximately 50 (W.-N. Lee et al., 2007; Praet, 2009) to 70% (Hagiwara et al., 2009; Mooney, 2000) of Japanese advertisements. However, in the context of older people, only a few studies mention the use of older celebrities at all (Hajjar, 1997; Higgs & Milner, 2006; Simcock & Sudbury, 2006; Y. B. Zhang et al., 2006), and nearly none of these studies investigates the phenomenon itself

(Yoon & Powell, 2012). Thus, this study will give insights into the usage of older celebrities.

Image of older people

A few studies on older people have analyzed the image of older people. This variable is important to understand if older people are portrayed in positive or in negative ways. Most studies have found that older people were more often portrayed positively than negatively (Langmeyer, 1993; Ong & Chang, 2009; Roy & Harwood, 1997; Simcock & Sudbury, 2006; Zimmerman, 2001). Langmeyer (1993) found that older people were being described as helping, knowledgeable, happy, and confident. Lee and associates (2007) had similar results, finding that older people were associated mostly with positive attributes such as "active," "happy," and "healthy." Roy and Harwood (1997) reported that older people were generally depicted positively and were featured as strong, active, happy, and lucid (not confused). Similar findings were also true in an East Asian context, where Ong and Chang (2009) found that more than 70% of older people in South Korean advertisements were depicted as happy, lucid, emotionally strong, and active; this was found to a much lesser extent in Malaysian advertisements. In contrast, Sudbury-Riley and Idris (2013) found more than one-third of older people who were sad, depressed, or unhappy. Finally, Peterson and Ross (1997) observed that while older people were more often depicted favorably than unfavorably, younger models were portrayed more favorably than older ones. In the 45–64 age group 66% of people were shown in a desirable way, while only 54% of people 65 years and older were shown favorably. Similarly, 34% of people in the age segment 45–64 years were shown in an undesirable way, while the same was true for 46% of the age group 65 years and older.

Social interaction

As with previous representations, the perceived value of older people may be inferred from the depiction of their social interactions. Considering whether older people are shown alone or together with other age groups, and identifying the groups they interact with, is important. Though the categories varied, most studies concluded that older people appear with age groups other than their own in more than 70% of advertisements (Greco, 1993; Roy & Harwood,

1997). Greco (1993) reported older people in multiple age groups in 78% of advertisements in 1985 and 70% of advertisements in 1990, while only 14% appeared alone in 1985 and 22% in 1990. Similarly, Roy and Harwood (1997) found 76.4% of older people appear with multiple age groups and only 13.0% appear exclusively with other older characters. Prieler (2008a) reports similar findings in a Japanese context. He found that older people are shown with multiple age groups; most commonly they appear with those aged 30–59 years. Additionally, he found that in cases where older people do appear alone it is nearly always for products that are clearly targeted at them, such as dentures, diapers for older people, hearing aids, food supplements, and anti-wrinkle creams. These findings may imply that older people are not regarded as valuable enough to appear only with members of their own age group but that other age groups must generally appear with them.

Setting

Another important variable for the content analysis of social groups is setting (Furnham & Mak, 1999), which may convey to television audiences that the lives of older people are confined to certain settings and connected activities. Surprisingly, this category has only scarcely been studied in previous research that analyses the portrayal of older people. The few findings in this area are mixed. Some research has found that more than half of advertisements with older people are in home settings (Swayne & Greco, 1987), which may be in line with the stereotype of older people not being active and mostly staying at home. For example, Swayne and Greco (1987) found home settings in 56% of advertisements, followed by business settings in 18%. However, other research has found that older people are predominantly in outside settings (Ong & Chang, 2009; T. Robinson, 1998). For example, Robinson (1998) reported 63% of older people were in outside settings, while only 8.7% were in home settings; these findings were consistent with magazines but not with newspapers where the home setting was dominant.

Product categories

The products associated with particular social groups indicate the preoccupations, competencies, and values of those associated with them (Mastro & Stern, 2003). For example, the strong association between women and cosmetic products emphasizes the importance society assigns to female beauty and contributes to their sexualization (Luyt, 2011). Needless to say, such limited portrayals lead to a distorted knowledge of various social groups. Older people in television advertisements, for their part, are most often used to promote foods/beverages. This is true for the United States (Atkins et al., 1990/1991; Greco, 1993; B.-K. Lee et al., 2006; M. M. Lee et al., 2007; D. W. Miller, Leyell, & Mazachek, 2004; Roy & Harwood, 1997), the United Kingdom (Simcock & Sudbury, 2006), South Korea (B.-K. Lee et al., 2006), and China (Y. B. Zhang et al., 2008). Other product categories that feature older people are financial/insurance (B.-K. Lee et al., 2006; Ong & Chang, 2009; Prieler, 2008a), and medication/health (Atkins et al., 1990/1991; M. M. Lee et al., 2007; Ong & Chang, 2009; T. Robinson, 1998).

Results

The results of this study are based on a sample which is drawn from a database of television advertisements that includes all advertisements being broadcast for the first time on any given day in the Greater Tokyo Area on the five commercial television stations and consists of 1,495 unduplicated television advertisements in 1997 and 1,477 in 2007: 2,972 in total. For further details about the method and sample, see Appendix 1.

We used chi-square analyses that were executed on a sample of unduplicated television advertisements that included people. Because we were interested in both the overall significant differences between 1997 and 2007 for each category, and which subcategories contributed to this significance, we broke the results down even further using the adjusted standardized residuals (ASRs) for post-hoc tests. In turn, we will try to analyze the results for each variable while simultaneously addressing the question regarding possible changes between the years 1997 and 2007.

Our content analysis showed an unequal age distribution within advertisements featuring people (see Table 3.1). The 15–34 age group clearly dominates, followed by the 35–49 age group. Age groups 50–64 and 65+ are only minimally present in Japanese advertisements. The same is true for the age group 0–14. It is striking that the distribution in 1997 and 2007 is overall very similar. However,

Table 3.1 Age distribution in Japanese advertisements and population census

Year of TV ads / Census	0–14 year %	15–34 years %	35–49 years %	50–64 years %	65+ years %
TV Ads 1997[a]	19.3	66.3	37.9	13.7	4.6
TV Ads 2007[b]	19.8	64.2	39.3	21.4	6.1
Census 1995[c]	16.0	28.2	21.9	19.4	14.6
Census 2005[c]	13.8	25.1	19.3	21.7	20.2

Notes:
[a] Number of all ads with people = 1,236. Different age groups in one advertisement possible.
[b] Number of all ads with people = 1,220. Different age groups in one advertisement possible.
[c] Percentages of the census are based on Ministry of Internal Affairs and Communications (1995, 2005).
The age distribution in the 2005 census and the 2007 TV advertisements are not perfectly comparable since the TV ads amount to more than 100% (due to the fact that different age groups can coexist in one advertisement).

there is one major exception, namely the age group 50–64, which increased by 56.2% from 13.7% to 21.4% Also, the 65+ age group increased by 32.6%.

These results already tell us a great deal about the changes between 1997 and 2007 as well as about what age groups are preferred in Japanese advertisements. A comparison with the population census gives better insight into a possible under- or overrepresentation of age groups (see Table 3.1). There are some clearly visible findings: the age groups 15–34 and 35–49 are overrepresented, and the age group 65+, which actually increased even more in the census than in the television advertisements (namely by 38.4%), is underrepresented in Japanese television advertisements.

There are proportional differences between men and women within different age groups (see Figure 3.1). Whereas for the 1–14 age group there are only slightly more women (n = 161) than men (n = 149) in the 2007 television advertisements, in the 15–34 age group women (n = 617) clearly outnumber men (n = 370). The situation, however, changes drastically after the age of 35, when men (n = 339) start dominating Japanese advertisements and women (n = 260) become subordinate. This is especially pronounced in the age group 50–64, where men are featured (n = 199) twice as often as women (n = 96). The same is true for the age group 65+, where men (n = 54) again clearly outnumber women (n = 29). This is even more noteworthy considering the fact that in Japanese society older women actually outnumber older men. This is the case with the 50+ age group, where the number of women exceeds men at a ratio of 1.18:1; as well as with the 65+ age group, where women outnumber men at a ratio of 1.36:1 at the closest census to our recordings (based on Ministry of Internal Affairs and Communications, 2005).

The overall percentages between 1997 and 2007 are rather similar, so the results from 1997 will not be displayed here. In terms of older people, however, it is worth mentioning that the number of men strongly increased, whereas the number of women decreased. The number of women in the 50–64 age bracket increased slightly (from 5.8%/n = 72 to 7.9%/n = 96), which does not match the growth of appearances by men of the same age (from 9.0%/n = 111 to 16.3%/n = 199). Similarly, the number of women aged 65 and over decreased

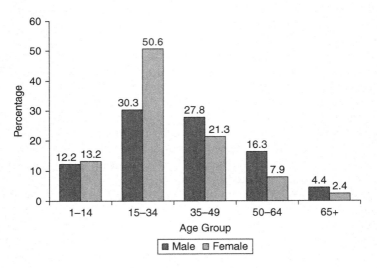

Figure 3.1   Age and sex distribution in Japanese advertisements

Note: Percentage of advertisements featuring males and females within all advertisements featuring people in 2007 (*N* = 1,220) – male and female and different age groups together in one advertisement possible.

(from 2.8%/n = 35 to 2.4%/n = 29), whereas the number of their male counterparts increased (from 2.9%/n = 36 to 4.4%/n = 54). This led to a lower number of women in all advertisements featuring older people. The fact that the number of older women decreased from 1997 to 2007 runs against the overall trend of more older people appearing in Japanese television advertisements, and necessitates further investigation.

Since the number of people 65 years or older is rather small, we have merged for the analysis of the following variables the 50–64 and the 65+ age categories. In the following we investigated the perceived importance of older people by analyzing the roles in which older people most frequently appear. In Japanese television advertisements, older people were shown predominantly in major roles (65.4% in 1997; 65.4% in 2007), followed by minor roles (30.3% and 28.8%); in a few cases, older people playing different roles appeared together in one television advertisement (4.3% and 5.9%; see Table 3.2). There were also more advertisements with older people playing major roles rather than minor roles. The results for roles were consistent between 1997 and 2007 ($\chi^2 = 0.669$, $df = 2$, $p = .716$).

Further analysis of older people in major roles, whether they are celebrities or not, showed that the majority of television advertisements featured celebrities in 1997 (65.7%) and in 2007 (61.2%) and thus little difference between the two years.

We then examined the image of older people in television advertisements and asked whether older people are predominantly portrayed in favorable or unfavorable ways. Older people were depicted more often in favorable ways (30.3% in 1997 and 39.2% in 2007) than in unfavorable ways (13.0% and 11.1%). Many advertisements could not be coded in one way or the other and were thus coded as "neither" (56.7% and 49.7%). Overall, there was no significant difference between the image of older people in 1997 and 2007 ($\chi^2 = 4.311$, $df = 2$, $p = .116$). Examining changes in the subcategories using adjusted standardized residuals (ASR), however, indicated that there was a significant change for the favorable image subcategory (ASR = ±2.1) which increased from 30.3% to 39.2% from 1997 to 2007.

In the following we investigated the age groups with which older people were predominantly depicted. There was a significant change in this respect between the two years ($\chi^2 = 19.781$, $df = 4$, $p = .001$). Older people were most often shown with adults younger than

Table 3.2 Roles, image, social interactions, settings, and product categories associated with older people

	1997 (N = 208) %	2007 (N = 306) %	χ^2
Role			
Major Role	65.4	65.4	0.669, $df = 2$, $p = .716$
Minor Role	30.3	28.8	
Both	4.3	5.9	
Image			
Favorable	30.3	39.2*	4.311, $df = 2$, $p = .116$
Neither	56.7	49.7	
Unfavorable	13.0	11.1	
Social Interaction			
Alone	20.2	38.2***	19.781, $df = 4$, $p = .001$
Older People	10.1	8.8	
Adults (younger than 50)	57.7	42.5***	
Child(ren)	2.9	3.3	
Multiple Generations	9.1	7.2	
Setting			
Home (inside)	20.2	17.3	11.004, $df = 4$, $p = .027$
Workplace (inside)	7.2	13.1*	
Other Inside	34.1	41.5	
Outside	25.5	17.0*	
Other (artificial, unclear, etc.)	13.0	11.1	
Product Categories			
Foods/ Beverages	23.1	25.8	6.889, $df = 9$, $p = .649$
Services/ Leisure	11.1	9.2	
Cosmetics/ Toiletries	9.1	10.1	
Distribution/ Retailing	8.7	9.5	
Pharmaceuticals/ Medical Supplies	8.2	4.2	
Real Estate/ Housing	7.2	5.6	
Finance/ Insurance	6.2	7.2	
Household Products	5.8	3.9	
Home Electric Appliance/AV Equipment	4.8	4.9	
Other[a]	15.9	19.6	

Notes:
* $p < .05$;** $p < .01$;*** $p < .001$
The significance levels for differences between subcategories are based on post-hoc tests using adjusted standardized residuals.
[a] The product categories automobile/related products, apparel/fashion/accessories/ personal items, precision instruments/office supplies, publications, and materials were added to the "other" product category due to low cell counts.

50 years old. This finding was true in 57.7% of the advertisements in 1997 and 42.5% in 2007. Though a significant decline occurred in the number of times older people appeared in advertisements with adults younger than 50 between 1997 and 2007 (ASR = ±3.4), it was still the dominant category for both years, especially when compared to the number of times older people appeared with other older people (10.1% and 8.8%). There was no significant change in the incidence of older people appearing with their own age group between 1997 and 2007 (ASR = ±.5). The incidence of older people shown alone did increase, however (20.2% for 1997; and 38.2% for 2007; ASR = ±4.3).

The settings in which older people were portrayed in television advertising changed significantly between the two years (χ^2 = 11.004, df = 4, p = .027). Older people appeared predominantly in other inside settings, such as restaurants (34.1% and 41.5%). Outside settings were the second-most common setting (25.5% and 17.0%), though this significantly decreased (ASR = ±2.3). Home settings placed third with 20.2% in 1997 and 17.3% in 2007. Workplace settings ranked fourth, but increased significantly from 7.2% to 13.1% (ASR = ±2.1). Finally, older people were also shown in other settings, such as artificial backgrounds (13.0% and 11.1%).

Finally, we analyzed with which product category older people are commonly portrayed. Older people were in advertisements mostly for foods/beverages (23.1% in 1997 and 25.8% in 2007) and services/leisure (11.1% and 9.2%). These categories were followed by cosmetics/toiletries (9.1% and 10.1%) and distribution/retailing (8.7% and 9.5%). Overall, the results for product categories were similar for both years (χ^2 = 6.889, df = 9, p = .649).

Discussion

Our research revealed an increase in advertisements featuring older people between 1997 and 2007. This was true for the 50–64 age group (13.7% to 21.4%) and the 65+ age group (4.6% to 6.1%). This increase reflects the increasing number of people in Japanese society who are 50 years or older and their importance in the Japanese marketplace. The increasing depiction of older people in television advertising is a reflection of society and shows that older people enjoy rising importance and presence in society, albeit still low overall. However, in the context of demographic reality, older people were significantly underrepresented in both years, though slightly less in 2007 than in 1997. This underrepresentation of older people is also in accordance with other media in other countries (Gerbner, 1993; Gunter, 1998; Harwood, 2007; Kessler, Rakoczy, & Staudinger, 2004; Signorielli, 2004).

While our results were in accordance with the majority of studies in the past 30 years, the fact that older people were still significantly underrepresented in our 2007 sample is striking given their importance in both demographic reality and in the Japanese marketplace. This underrepresentation is even more surprising considering that around 60% of older people were celebrities and because our definition of older people, which included people 50 years of age or older, was rather broad. In addition, there has been an influential body of literature claiming that Japanese people highly respect older people (e.g., Palmore & Maeda, 1985) based on the traditional dominance of Confucianism which demands respect toward older people (O'Leary, 1993). However, there is substantial empirical evidence to the contrary (Koyano, 1989; Levy, 1999) which debunks these myths of the "honorable elder" in Japan (Koyano, 1997; Tsuji, 1997). Overall, it seems that negative images of old age prevail in Japan (Formanek, 2008), or at least that both positive and negative views exist at the same time (Hagiwara et al., 2009).

In addition to cultural reasons, there may be other explanations for the underrepresentation of older people in advertising. As some researchers have suggested, advertising agencies generally believe that older models alienate younger consumers. In the United Kingdom and the United States the advertising industry itself has a rather youthful profile (Greco, 1989; Szmigin & Carrigan, 2000a) and young people are usually not able to imagine the world of older consumers (McCaughan, 2015; Nyren, 2007). Additionally, older people tend to identify with people five to ten years younger than themselves (Barak, 2009; Moschis & Mathur, 2006; Stephens, 1991; Sudbury-Riley et al., 2015) and thus respond better to younger models than those of the same age as them (Greco, 1989). This is also true in Japan (Kohlbacher & Chéron, 2012; Prieler et al., 2015). Regardless of the reasons for the underrepresentation of older people, its effects on the television audience could result in an assumption that older people are only a small part of the population with little importance and relevance to society (Gerbner, Gross, Morgan, & Signorielli, 1981). The underrepresentation of older people in advertising might also reflect the fact that older people still do not have enough powerful support groups in Japan (Abrams et al., 2003).

In both 1997 and 2007 the representation of older men in advertisements clearly outnumbered the representation of older women. This is a finding common to nearly all studies worldwide (Furnham & Mak, 1999). The percentage of older women represented even decreased between 1997 and 2007 for the age group 65 years or older (from 2.8% to 2.4%). This is a surprising result, given that older women outnumber and outlive men in Japan. However, this finding confirms that negative attitudes toward older women still exist in Japan (Formanek, 2008). This misrepresentation and underrepresentation of older women has real consequences in that it can shape society's attitudes toward older women (Gerbner, 1998; Gerbner et al., 1980). For example, people might learn through such representations that older women are not as valuable as older men and as younger women (Bandura, 2009).

Although our research shows that older men clearly outnumber older women, older men are also underrepresented overall. For women, however, underrepresentation is much more pronounced: the number of advertisements featuring older women was half that of those with older men. In Japanese advertising, like in other countries, there is a strong preference for young and beautiful women (Arima, 2003; Yamanaka, 2000). Suzuki (1995) explains: "The reason that women in lower age brackets are used is that the highest value accorded to women in Japan is that they be young and 'cute' or 'beautiful'" (p. 79). The result is that older women become invisible while their younger counterparts are celebrated, a fact that corroborates Roy and Harwood's (1997) claim in a US context that "societal sexism extends, indeed perhaps intensifies, through the lifespan" (p. 5). Some researchers have called this attitude the "double standard of aging," or the concept that society is much more permissive about aging in men than in women (Sontag, 1972). In Japan particularly, women are selected for television based mostly on youth and looks, while in the case of men it is based on standing, experience, and education (Suzuki, 1995).

The fact that television advertisements in Japan do not represent demographic realities is not surprising, since this is the case

in most countries. While this is not a problem in itself, "the important question is not so much whether there are deviations, but what
kind exist, and with what consequences for thinking and action"
(Gerbner et al., 1980, p. 42). The deviations here have real consequences in that they perpetuate an unfortunate combination of
ageism and sexism – a combination that influences the audience's
images of older women (Bandura, 2009; Gerbner, 1998). What is true
for Mastro and Stern's (2003) work in the United States is also true
for this study: "Perhaps the most blatant message viewers might take
away from this age distribution is that young women are particularly important to our society, and that youth is less important for
men than it is for women" (p. 21). By the same token, older women
seem to have very little social importance. This is a finding that is,
however, not only true for advertising, but was also found to be true
in other media (Bazzini, McIntosh, Smith, Cook, & Harris, 1997;
Gerbner, 1993; Kessler et al., 2004).

While cultural respect for older people did not affect their
frequency of representation in advertising, respect for older people
might appear in other ways, as in the case of the roles they play.
In both 1997 and 2007, older people in Japanese television advertisements usually played major roles. This is in contrast to several
previous studies conducted in the United States and the United
Kingdom (Greco, 1993; Roy & Harwood, 1997; Simcock & Sudbury,
2006), though it is in accordance with studies on East Asia (B.-K.
Lee et al., 2006; Ong & Chang, 2009). These findings, including our
own, may result from the fact that East Asian cultures are based on
Confucian values which stipulate the importance and special status
of older people within society. While this status might not lead to
a higher number of older people in advertisements, it could mean
that they will be represented in more important roles than in the
West. However, this is only one way to interpret the data. Another
possible reason is that more than 60% of older people in both years
were celebrities, and celebrities are commonly shown in major
roles. As other research has shown, celebrities can be a good way
for representing older people in advertising (Yoon & Powell, 2012).
Whatever the reasons, the predominance of older people in major
roles may show the actual importance of older people in society
as stated by ethnolinguistic vitality theory (Abrams et al., 2003;
Harwood & Anderson, 2002). This may in turn teach the audience

about their importance in society, as suggested by social cognitive theory (Bandura, 2009).

While there were no significant changes in older people's perceived importance between the two years (1997 and 2007), there were changes in the image of older people. There was a larger number of older people portrayed favorably in 2007 than in 1997 (39.2% vs. 30.3%). This change seems to be in accordance with the theory that television advertisements reflect changes in society and culture. The general findings of more favorable depictions in both years are in accordance with previous research in countries such as the United States, the United Kingdom, South Korea, and Malaysia (Langmeyer, 1993; Ong & Chang, 2009; Roy & Harwood, 1997; Simcock & Sudbury, 2006; Zimmerman, 2001). However, our results must also be observed in the context of the finding by Peterson and Ross (1997), who observed that younger models within the older age segment were portrayed more favorably than older ones, and also that our sample employs predominantly younger models within the older age segment (i.e., 50–64 years). In short, there were obvious changes in the image of older people between the two years. However, the majority of depictions of older people were neither favorable nor unfavorable, but neutral. This is another significant finding of our research and our contribution to the state of the field. Previous research has focused only on binary variables (favorable vs. unfavorable), which does not tell the whole story of representations of older people in Japanese television advertisements.

There was also a significant change in the social interactions of older people in advertisements between the two study years. Our results on the social interaction between older people and other age groups were in accordance with previous studies which found that older people appear predominantly with people other than their own age group in advertisements. However, while previous studies found that older people appeared with people other than those in their own age group more than 70% of the time (Greco, 1993; Roy & Harwood, 1997), we found far fewer examples of this. In contrast to Robinson (1998), our study did not find increased instances of older people portrayed with their own age group, but rather that older people were increasingly shown alone (20.2% for 1997; 38.2% for 2007). Our results are in strong contrast to all previous studies investigating this variable and thus may point toward the increasing importance of older people in Japan. In the past, television advertisements rarely depicted an older person alone; instead, older people usually appeared in multi-generational groups. However, this situation has changed, which may indicate greater importance of older people in Japanese society.

This study has found inside settings such as restaurants to be the most predominant setting for advertisements featuring older people. This finding requires further research because previously strong categories such as home and outside ranked only second and third, respectively. It suggests that older people were generally depicted as active and not sitting passively at home. Outside settings and other inside settings are connected with forms of activity. Relatedly, there was a significant increase in the use of the workplace setting between 1997 and 2007, revealing an overall trend of depicting older people as more active. This characterization might be connected with the increasingly aging workforce in Japan (Kohlbacher, 2011; Kohlbacher & Mollenhauer, 2013). Overall, these representations of active older people might show the audience that older people are still active members of Japanese society and not passive, as some stereotypes about them suggest. These findings, however, must be observed in the context of our sample, which predominantly contained individuals from the 50–64 age group.

Our study has also confirmed previous research in other countries on product categories associated with older people in television advertisements: foods/beverages clearly dominated our sample. A reason for this commonality might be that within food advertisements, multiple generations are especially common since the producers want to emphasize that all generations will enjoy the product (Prieler, 2008a). Other reasons might be the general importance of food in Japan and the credibility of older models, especially in advertising for traditional products. The dominance of foods/beverages within our sample, however, must be seen in perspective, since this product category is also overall the strongest in Japanese television advertising, as shown in previous work (Hagiwara et al., 2009). The results that we found for product categories such as service/leisure, cosmetics/toiletries, and distribution/retailing are not in line with previous research. In contrast to previous research, the product categories typically associated with older people, such as the medication/health products category, were not found to be associated with older people in this study. This finding might be connected with the fact that the majority of our advertisements included older people in the 50–64 age group for whom medication and health products are less important than for older cohorts.

Implications

As this chapter has shown, there were several changes in Japanese advertising between 1997 and 2007 that may reflect the increasing importance of older people within Japanese society. The increasing appearances of older people in advertising in primarily major roles, alone and in the workplace, may suggest this increase in importance. Additionally, the increasing favorable depiction of older people shows a change in how older people are portrayed. Japanese advertising agencies apparently have come to understand and adapt to the fact that older people have become an important force within Japanese society and are a prominent market segment.

However, the situation has yet to come to maturity and it remains to be seen if legislation is necessary, as some scholars have previously suggested (e.g., Carrigan & Szmigin, 2000b). Even though the number of television advertisements with older people has increased, in 2007 older people were still highly underrepresented, especially older women. This is an area where advertisements still have to improve, since watching television advertisements is also a way to learn about older people (Bandura, 2009). The current underrepresentation of older people might lead to misconceptions and negative attitudes about older people by all age groups (Haboush, Warren, & Benuto, 2012) and could also lead to the development of a negative self-image among older people (e.g., feeling denied by society) (Donlon et al., 2005; Gerbner et al., 1980; Mares & Cantor, 1992) and might even affect their well-being (Garstka & Schmitt, 2004). Advertising agencies might see this as a purely social issue; however, the representation of older people also has an influence on whether or not an audience likes an advertisement, the company image, and the consumer's intentions for purchasing products and services (Festervand & Lumpkin, 1985; Kohlbacher, Prieler, et al., 2011a; Kolbe & Burnett, 1992; T. Robinson, Gustafson, & Popovich,

2008). Thus, advertising agencies should be more concerned about the social responsibility of advertisements and also employ more older advertising practitioners who can better understand that age group (McCaughan, 2015; Nyren, 2007).

4
Advertising Practitioners' Views on the Use of Older Models

This chapter looks at advertising practitioners' views on the use of older models in advertising in Japan (see also: Hagiwara et al., 2010; Kohlbacher, Prieler, & Hagiwara, 2011b, 2014). Our content analysis of television advertising (Chapter 3) seems to suggest that advertising agencies are relatively reluctant to feature older models, especially those who are non-celebrities, as well as those who are 65 years and older. However, the content analysis can only serve as an indirect indication of advertising practitioners' views and attitudes and does not reveal the reasons for their decision not to use many older models. We have therefore decided to ask advertising practitioners directly through qualitative interviews and a questionnaire-based survey.

As mentioned in Chapter 1, the major Japanese advertising agencies have set up specialized departments to study older consumers (Dentsu Senior Project, 2007; Hakuhodo, 2003) as a consequence of the demographic shift. Choosing the right models and portraying them appropriately are crucial tasks in marketing management and advertising creation (Lynch & Schuler, 1994), and research shows that the way in which older television viewers feel represented by a company in its advertisements has an influence on the overall company image and purchase intentions (see also Chapter 5, Festervand & Lumpkin, 1985; Kohlbacher, Prieler et al., 2011a, 2011b; Kolbe & Burnett, 1992; T. Robinson et al., 2003). Additionally, there are potential negative effects of consumers' comparisons with models in advertisements (Richins, 1991), and advertisements which consumers find congruent with their self-concept are more effective in terms of brand preference and purchase intention (Hoffmann et al., 2012; Hong & Zinkhan, 1995). Indeed, this so-called self-congruity effect between brand personalities and targeted consumers' self-concepts has been shown to be rather strong and robust (Aguirre-Rodriguez et al., 2012). Therefore, one important consideration is how and with which models older people are addressed. This may also have implications for corporate social responsibility in terms of the portrayal of these models or spokespersons (cf. Carrigan & Szmigin, 2000b; Kohlbacher, Prieler et al., 2011b; Peterson & Ross, 1997).

Most accounts of advertising in the aging society so far have analyzed consumers and their reactions toward the portrayal of older people in advertising (see Chapter 5) or used content analysis to investigate the representation of older people in advertisements (see Chapter 3). However, despite its obvious importance, previous research on the perceptions of advertising practitioners on the use of older models in advertising is scarce. A thorough review of the literature revealed that there are only two empirical studies that have been reported to date. The first one is a study conducted by Greco (1988, 1989) in the United States and its replication in the United Kingdom by Szmigin and Carrigan (2000a).

The small number of studies and the fact that they were conducted many years ago combined with the rising importance of demographic changes, show the urgent need for further empirical research (Kohlbacher et al., 2014). This chapter presents results from a survey of advertising practitioners in Japan. Our research is a replication and, more importantly, an extension of the previous research. Replications and extensions play a valuable role in ensuring the integrity of a discipline's empirical results and are considered to be important for the advancement of science (Hubbard & Armstrong, 1994; Madden, Easley, & Dunn, 1995). In fact, there is a need to replicate previous research to validate the findings and to determine facts (Easley, Madden, & Dunn, 2000; Hunter, 2001), and there have been calls to reinstate replication as an important component of advertising research (Berthon, Ewing, Pitt, & Berthon, 2003). We follow this call by replicating and extending Greco's (1988) study in a different context. The different context is given by a different time (more than 25 years later) and different country (Japan) which is in line with one of the replication strategies outlined by Berthon and associates (2003).

Our study is also more fine-grained than previous research, as it distinguishes between two groups of older people/spokespersons (50–64 years vs. 65 years or older), and the survey is much larger than the previous two. As our study focuses on the attitudes of advertising practitioners about the communication objectives and effectiveness of older spokespersons, their general views on older models in advertising, and the effectiveness of older models by product category, it also contributes to the knowledge about Japanese advertising practices more generally and thus also to international advertising (cf. Cui, Liu, Yang, & Wang, 2013).

Literature review

As pointed out in Chapter 1, older people are playing an increasingly important role in society (Akiyama, 2010; Coulmas, 2007; Kohlbacher, 2011) based on the rapid aging of Japan's population and the consequent strong increase of older cohorts – both in absolute as well as relative terms. It is especially their economic impact that can be widely felt, as workers, consumers, and target segments (Dentsu Senior Project, 2007; Hakuhodo, 2003; Kohlbacher, 2011; Kohlbacher & Chéron, 2012; Murata, 2012).

According to the audience-as-commodity model (Smythe, 1977; Webster & Phalen, 1997) audiences are products, and advertisers are consumers of that audience product, which means that advertisers – as consumers – seek audiences that provide them with the greatest utility at the lowest cost, relative to other options and given their budget constraints (Coffey, 2013; Hoskins, McFayden, & Finn, 2004). This utility or audience value depends on the unique, differentiable traits of each audience (Coffey, 2013) and given the audience size and income of older people in Japan, their audience value is obviously very high, which makes them an attractive target segment for advertisers. As a result, advertisers and advertising practitioners should also treat older people well in their television advertisements in order to create a positive relationship with them.

However, in reality thus far marketing as well as advertising practitioners have been criticized for stereotyping older people, focusing too much on younger age segments, neglecting older consumers, and considering them only for such items as denture cleansers, laxatives, arthritic remedies, and other products that are clearly designed to relieve the aches and pains of old age (e.g., Bartos, 1980; Carrigan & Szmigin, 1999; cf. also Yoon & Powell, 2012 for a review of the literature). As outlined in Chapter 3, content analyses on the representation of older people in advertising have confirmed such findings for magazines (P. N. Miller, Miller, McKibbin, & Pettys, 1999; Ursic, Ursic, & Ursic, 1986; Zhou & Chen, 1992) and television (Kessler et al., 2010; Prieler et al., 2015; Simcock & Sudbury, 2006; Swayne & Greco, 1987) in various countries.

While content analytical studies offer valuable insights and contribute to our understanding of the role of older people in advertising, they can only speculate about the reasons behind their findings (such as the underrepresentation of older people). Summarizing previous research, Milliman and Erffmeyer (1990) found four general explanations for the tendency to use younger models in advertising: first, the sentiment that young people hold a negative attitude toward older people; second, the idea that older models are "poor copy" in advertisements; third, the fact that people attach negative descriptions to older models; and fourth, advertisers may fear negative reactions to older models in advertisements from the younger segments of the market. Unfortunately, Milliman and Erffmeyer do not provide any empirical evidence to support their claims. Research on the perceptions of advertising practitioners on the use of older models in advertising is thus necessary to shed more light onto these issues.

However, in contrast to content analyses and studies on consumer reactions to older models that are abundant, there are only two studies on the perceptions of advertising practitioners on the use of older models. The first one is a study conducted by Greco (1988, 1989) in the United States. The second one is a replication in the United Kingdom by Szmigin and Carrigan (2000a). Greco (1988) found that in general, advertising executives feel that it is possible for older spokespersons to get an audience's attention and help gain awareness for new products, while there is generally less agreement that an older spokesperson enhances message comprehension. Advertising practitioners further indicated that older spokespersons can aid in persuasion and serve to enhance source credibility, while only a smaller number of them felt that older spokespersons help to gain action or purchase of the product (Greco, 1988). In terms of product categories, the respondents most often recommended older spokespersons for health and medicines if the target audience was also older consumers. While older spokespersons were also deemed appropriate for, among other products, travel and vacations, financial services, insurance, rental property, hotels, and food, this was not the case for clothing, cosmetics, and shampoo, for example (Greco, 1988, 1989).

In their replication in the United Kingdom, Szmigin and Carrigan (2000a) obtained only 19 fully completed questionnaires and found that advertising executives were cautious about recommending the use of older models in their advertising executions, but agreed that the frequency of use of older people as central figures would increase during the next couple of years. In terms of product categories, health and medicine and financial services were the only two categories for which the majority of the respondents would recommend using older models as central figures in their advertisements (Szmigin & Carrigan, 2000a). They finally concluded that part of the explanation for the lack of representation of older people in advertising has less to do with their "unsuitability" and more to do with ingrained stereotypical prejudice on the part of many advertisers (Szmigin & Carrigan, 2000a).

Based on the very small number of studies on perceptions of advertising practitioners of older models, which were conducted a long time ago in countries with very distinct cultures from Japan, our research takes the approach of exploring some questions based on previous research. We try to analyze the questions of whether the opinions of advertising practitioners about communication objectives and effectiveness are generally positive or negative; if their general views on older models are positive or negative; which factors determine their intention to use older models; for which product categories is advertising practitioners' perceived effectiveness of older models the highest (and if this varies by intended audience – that is, older audience versus general audience); and if these perceptions vary if older models are defined as 65+ versus 50–64 years of age.

Indeed, while Greco's (1988, 1989) study focused on "elderly" spokespersons aged 65 years and older, Szmigin and Carrigan (2000a) defined "older" models as 50 and above. As outlined in Chapter 1, we distinguish between two segments or types of older consumers and older models in this research: one defining older models/spokespersons as 50–64 and another one as 65+, which is an important contribution of our research to distinguish between the younger and the older part of the market for older people. We will therefore also check whether advertising practitioners' views differ if the model/ spokesperson is defined as 65+ in comparison to 50–64 years of age.

Results

The results of this study are based on a large sample survey of advertising practitioners (N=185) in Japan in July and August 2009. Respondents ranged in age from 23 to 66 (M=46.87, SD=10.313), were predominantly male (86.9%) and had an average of 21.28 years (Min=1, Max=44, Mdn=22) of work experience in the advertising industry. For further details about the method and the sample, see Appendix 2.

Attitudes in terms of communication objectives and effectiveness of older spokespersons

At first we analyzed the attitudes of advertising practitioners about older spokespersons in terms of their communication objectives and effectiveness. Table 4.1 presents the percentages of those who agreed or strongly agreed to each attitudinal statement in comparison to the percentages of those who disagreed or strongly disagreed as well as the mean and standard deviation.

The items are arranged in descending order of the mean value. All one-sample t-tests were significant on the 5% level (not shown), thus indicating that all means were significantly higher than the mid-point value of three (i.e., the respondents were agreeing with the statements). The same result was obtained when conducting the test with the summated scales against the "mid-point" of 24 (t=12.520(180), p<.001, 1-tailed for the 50–64 age group; t=11.279(179), p<.001, 1-tailed for the 65+ age group). These findings suggest that the attitudes of advertising practitioners about older spokespersons in terms of their communication objectives and effectiveness are positive.

Paired-samples t-tests between the means of the statements for the two different model age groups (50–64 vs. 65+) revealed statistically significant differences for only one item: "Mood with older spokespersons aids persuasion" (t=–2.24(184), p<.05, 1-tailed). This means that the level of agreement was higher for the older model age group

Table 4.1 Opinions about communication objectives and effectiveness for older spokespersons

	Older Model = 50–64 years				Older Model = 65+ years			
Statements	% DA/ SDA	% AG/ SAG	Mean	Stdv	% DA/ SDA	% AG/ SAG	Mean	Stdv
Mood with older spokespersons aids persuasion.	1.62	75.68	3.83	0.60	2.16	75.68	3.91	0.69
Older spokespersons help enhance source credibility.	3.78	63.78	3.66	0.66	4.32	62.70	3.69	0.71
Older spokespersons are effective at gaining comprehension.	3.83	39.34	3.37	0.59	4.92	40.44	3.38	0.63
Older spokespersons get the audience's attention.	4.89	38.59	3.34	0.58	5.43	40.76	3.40	0.67
Older spokespersons are effective for gaining intention to purchase.	4.86	32.97	3.29	0.60	5.95	33.51	3.31	0.67
Older spokespersons are effective in persuading audiences to switch brands.	9.78	27.72	3.20	0.67	11.96	25.54	3.16	0.75
Older spokespersons are effective for gaining purchase.	8.11	20.54	3.14	0.58	8.70	22.28	3.16	0.66
Older spokespersons help gain awareness of new products.	10.33	20.11	3.11	0.57	9.24	19.57	3.11	0.61

Note: DA/SGA=Disagree/Strongly Disagree; AG/SAG=Agree/Strongly Agree.

than for the younger model age group in this case. This is also the case for "Older spokespersons help enhance source credibility," even though not statistically significant.

Given that we found statistically significant differences for only one out of eight items, it does not seem to be the case that the opinions are more negative when the model/spokesperson is defined as 65+ in comparison to 50–64 years of age. This was also confirmed by a non-significant paired-samples t-test between the two summated scales (t=−1.121(179), p=.132, 1-tailed).

General views on older models in advertising

In the following we analyzed advertising practitioners' general views on older models in advertising (Table 4.2). Of the eight items analyzed, six had means above the mid-point value of three for both model age groups. One-sample t-tests revealed that these means were significantly higher than the mid-point for all of these six items except for one ("Older persons 'learn' how to behave from the portrayals of older characters seen in advertising"). The mean value of 3.04 for this item indicates that the respondents' opinions are rather neutral about this statement, that is, on average they opted for neither agree nor disagree.

As for the two items with a mean below three, one ("There are greater risks of negative effects on a general audience when older spokespersons are used") is not significantly lower than the mid-point – indicating neutrality – while the other ("Older spokespersons should be used in the advertising of products targeted to general audiences") is. That is, there is apparently a slight disagreement with this statement, indicating that advertising practitioners would not recommend using older spokespersons in the advertising of products targeted to general audiences.

The intention to use older models exists, even though it is not very strongly pronounced. Only 27% directly advocated the increased use of 50–64-year-old models and 28% for 65+ models in the future. However, while advertising practitioners say that a larger number of older people should be used, they are not fully of this opinion when targeting a general audience. Indeed, only 12% agreed for the 50–64 models and 10% for the 65+ models, while 20% or 22% respectively disagreed, with the majority being neutral. Also here, a significant difference between the age group of older

Table 4.2 General views on older models in advertising

Statements	Older Model = 50–64 years				Older Model = 65+ years			
	% DA/ SDA	% AG/ SAG	Mean	Stdv	% DA/ SDA	% AG/ SAG	Mean	Stdv
Intention to use older models								
More older persons should be used in advertising.	4.32	27.03	3.24	0.58	5.41	28.11	3.27	0.65
Older spokespersons should be used in the advertising of products targeted to general audiences.	19.57	11.96	2.90	0.62	22.28	9.78	2.84	0.64
Expected increase in older models in the future								
The amount of older models will increase during the next five years.	4.86	67.03	3.69	0.67	5.41	61.08	3.64	0.71
There will be an increased interest by clients to use older models during the next five years.	4.32	63.24	3.64	0.65	5.41	60.54	3.61	0.68
Perceived socialization effects of older models								
Older persons in advertising typically serve as role models for the older audience.	19.46	43.24	3.21	0.86	20.54	42.70	3.18	0.88
Older persons "learn" how to behave from the portrayals of older characters seen in advertising.	22.70	30.27	3.04	0.83	23.24	30.81	3.04	0.85
Perceived risks and problems of using older models								
Pre-testing ads containing the older is more important than pre-testing ads with younger characters.	16.22	41.08	3.27	0.87	15.76	44.57	3.35	0.95
There are greater risks of negative effects on a general audience when older spokespersons are used.	29.19	20.54	2.90	0.85	28.65	24.86	2.96	0.89

Note: DA/SGA=Disagree/Strongly Disagree; AG/SAG=Agree/Strongly Agree.

people is given. Advertising practitioners are more skeptical of the usage of older models to target a general audience if these models are 65 years or older (t=2.56(183); p<.05, 1-tailed). Summing the two items up to form an *intention to use older models scale*, we find that it is significantly above the "mid-point" of 6 for the 50–64 age group (t=1.92(183); p<.05, 1-tailed), but not for the 65+ age group (t=1.37(183); p=.09, 1-tailed). However, the means for the summated scale are not significantly different between the two age groups (t=0.74(183); p=.23, 1-tailed).

Advertising practitioners strongly expect an increased usage of older models, including an increased interest by clients to use them (with more than 60% of respondents agreeing with the statements and less than 6% disagreeing). The scales for both age groups are significantly above the mid-point. We see a significant difference between older people 65+ and ones in the age group of 50–64 years of age. There is a significant difference between the usage of these models when practitioners are asked about the increase of older models during the next five years (t=1.89(184); p<.05, 1-tailed), and the client's interest in the next few years (t=1.74(184); p<.05, 1-tailed), indicating that this expectation is higher for the 50–64 age group than for the 65+ age group. The difference between the two age groups is also significant for the summated scale (t=2.04(184); p<.05, 1-tailed).

Advertising practitioners agree to a certain extent regarding the socialization effects of advertisements. Forty-three percent agree that older models serve as role models to the older audience, while 30% believe that older people learn how to behave from the portrayal of older models in television advertisements. The scales for both age groups are significantly above the mid-point. The socialization effects are perceived to be the same for both the 50–64 and the 65+ age group (t=0.80(184); p=.21, 1-tailed).

Finally, advertising practitioners are aware of possible risks and problems involving older models. While they are rather neutral about possible negative effects of using older models on a general audience, they are of the opinion that pre-testing advertisements containing older people is more important than pre-testing advertisements with younger models. The perceived risks of using older models scale is significantly above the mid-point of 6 for the 65+ age group (t=2.61(183); p<.05, 1-tailed), but not for the 50–64 age group (t=1.60(184); p=.06, 1-tailed). For both questions, the level of agreement is significantly higher for the 65+ age group than for the 50–64 one (t=-2.56(184); p<.05, 1-tailed for the risks; t=-3.05(183); p<.001, 1-tailed for pre-testing; t=-3.96(183); p<.01, 1-tailed for the scale).

Factors influencing the intention to use more older models

Table 4.3 shows the results from a multiple regression which tries to predict the intention to use more older models and investigate which factors play a role. The overall model is statistically significant (F=14.21, p< .001 for the 50–64 age group; F=10.87, p< .001 for the 65+ age group). Of the four predictor variables, only two show a statistically significant impact on the intention to use more older models. The first is the "Perceived effectiveness of older spokespersons" and the second is "Expected increase in older models in the future." Both the betas (see Table 4.3) and the part correlations

Table 4.3 Multiple regression to predict effect on intentions to use more older models

Multiple Regression	50–64					65+				
Intention to use more older models	N=174					N=174				
	B	SE B	β	t	p	B	SE B	β	t	p
Constant	1.51	0.65	–	2.33	0.02	2.11	0.65	–	3.25	0.00
Perceived effectiveness of older spokespersons	0.11	0.02	0.34	4.83	0.00	0.09	0.02	0.30	4.27	0.00
Expected increase in older models in the future	0.16	0.05	0.22	3.14	0.00	0.22	0.05	0.29	4.10	0.00
Perceived socialization effects of older models	0.07	0.04	0.11	1.47	0.14	−0.03	0.05	−0.05	−0.63	0.53
Perceived risks and problems of using older models	0.01	0.04	0.02	0.32	0.75	0.04	0.05	0.06	0.87	0.39
Adjusted R^2	0.23					0.19				

(not shown) reveal that the former has a stronger influence than the latter. "Perceived socialization effects of older models" and "Perceived risks and problems of using older models" do not significantly predict the intention to use more older models. Overall, the predictors explain 23% of the variance in the case of the 50–64 age group and 19% in the case of the 65+ age group. We also ran the regression including a number of control variables but they did not have any significant impact: company size (sales, number of employees), age, gender, education, and years of industry experience of the respondent. We have also checked for interaction effects between the independent variables but found none. When checking for mediation, we found that "expected increase in older models in the future" mediates the relationship between "perceived effectiveness of older spokespersons" and "intention to use more older models" but the effect was very small.

Product categories and match-up hypothesis

Researchers determined a strong interaction between model age and product age-orientation, that is, youth-oriented products are best with young models and older-oriented products are best with older models (Rotfeld, Reid, & Wilcox, 1982). These observations are in line with the so-called *match-up hypothesis* which argues that some sort of congruence or match-up between the characteristics of the spokesperson in advertisements and the characteristics of the product advertised are important for achieving effectiveness (see e.g., H. Choi, Paek, & King, 2012; Kamins & Gupta, 1994; Lynch & Schuler, 1994; Paek, Nelson, & Vilela, 2011). Another "match-up effect" concerns the age congruity between the respondent and the advertisement model or spokesperson (Hoffmann et al., 2012; Oakes & North, 2011) as well as the perceived brand age (Huber, Meyer, Vogel, Weihrauch, & Hamprecht, 2013). For example, researchers found an identification of older consumers with older models (Nelson & Smith, 1988).

We analyzed advertising practitioners' perceptions of the effectiveness of older models by product category. Table 4.4 shows the responses to the effectiveness of older models by product category for the case of older people as a target group and Table 4.5 shows them for the case of a general audience as a target group.

Table 4.4 Effectiveness of older models by product category (target group: older people)

Target group is older people	Older Model = 50–64 years				Older Model = 65+ years			
Product categories	% DA/ SDA	% AG/ SAG	Mean	Stdv	% DA/ SDA	% AG/ SAG	Mean	Stdv
Health/Medical products and services/ Pharmaceuticals	1.09	87.50	4.07	0.63	4.35	80.98	3.96	0.72
Travel/Hotels	1.63	83.70	3.98	0.64	5.46	72.13	3.80	0.74
Financial services/ Insurance	2.73	71.58	3.81	0.68	8.74	56.83	3.56	0.78
Real estate/ Housing and interior goods	12.57	56.28	3.46	0.77	17.13	41.99	3.28	0.84
Services/Leisure/ Education	15.76	49.46	3.38	0.85	20.65	39.13	3.20	0.89
Publications/ Publishing	13.04	47.83	3.37	0.80	16.85	41.30	3.27	0.92
Foods/Beverages	15.85	41.53	3.28	0.78	20.22	30.60	3.12	0.84
Home electric appliances	13.04	36.96	3.27	0.76	19.67	28.96	3.10	0.83
Cosmetics	19.02	43.48	3.26	0.89	26.23	28.96	2.97	0.93
Automobiles	19.57	39.13	3.23	0.87	34.97	20.22	2.78	0.89
Sport products	26.63	39.13	3.12	0.94	34.97	26.23	2.85	0.94
Apparel/ Accessories	29.35	31.52	3.01	0.91	36.41	22.28	2.81	0.89
Cleansers/ Detergents	25.54	21.20	2.93	0.77	30.43	14.67	2.78	0.81

Note: DA/SGA=Disagree/Strongly Disagree; AG/SAG=Agree/Strongly Agree.

Figure 4.1 shows this perceived effectiveness of older models by product category graphically. Practitioners perceived the highest effectiveness of older models in health-related products regardless of the model's age if the target group is older people, but if the target group is a general audience, then the perceived effectiveness is highest for financial services/insurance. In comparison to other

Table 4.5 Effectiveness of older models by product category (target group: general audience)

Target group is a general audience	Older Model = 50–64 years				Older Model = 65+ years			
Product categories	% DA/ SDA	% AG/ SAG	Mean	Stdv	% DA/ SDA	% AG/ SAG	Mean	Stdv
Financial services/ Insurance	31.52	28.26	2.93	0.86	41.85	17.93	2.67	0.89
Real estate/ Housing and interior goods	33.88	18.03	2.80	0.82	48.90	11.54	2.53	0.86
Health/Medical products and services/ Pharmaceuticals	45.11	24.46	2.76	0.93	54.64	16.94	2.51	0.97
Publications/ Publishing	45.11	16.85	2.63	0.88	52.17	13.59	2.48	0.94
Travel/Hotels	53.80	18.48	2.58	0.90	60.87	12.50	2.35	0.92
Home electric appliances	51.37	9.84	2.47	0.84	59.02	5.46	2.27	0.85
Services/ Leisure/ Education	53.26	13.04	2.46	0.89	62.84	8.20	2.25	0.89
Automobiles	56.52	10.87	2.43	0.85	69.57	3.80	2.10	0.83
Foods/ Beverages	55.43	8.15	2.41	0.82	64.29	4.40	2.21	0.82
Cleansers/ Detergents	58.15	3.80	2.32	0.78	63.04	3.26	2.21	0.81
Sport products	66.30	7.61	2.21	0.87	74.32	4.92	2.03	0.86
Apparel/ Accessories	71.43	4.95	2.10	0.83	78.02	1.65	1.90	0.79
Cosmetics	72.83	6.52	2.08	0.87	79.89	3.80	1.89	0.83

Note: DA/SGA=Disagree/Strongly Disagree; AG/SAG=Agree/Strongly Agree.

product categories the perceived effectiveness of older models for foods/beverages is neither high nor low, regardless of model age and target group.

If we take health-related products as representative of age-oriented products and sports product categories as representative of youth-related product categories, then we can conclude that advertising practitioners' perceived effectiveness of older models are higher for age-oriented product categories than for youth-oriented product categories. This was confirmed for both

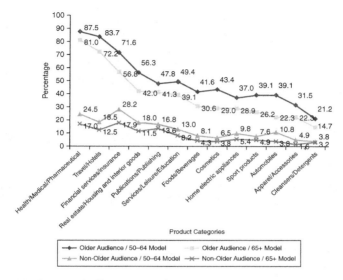

Figure 4.1   Perceived effectiveness of older models by product category

Note: Do you recommend using an older model? (Percentage of somewhat recommend and strongly recommend).

intended audiences and for both 50–64 years and 65+ models by paired-sample t-tests that all are significant at the 1%-level (not shown). Overall, advertising practitioners' perceived effectiveness of older models by product category is lower if the model/spokesperson was defined as 65+ in comparison to 50–64 years of age, regardless of the target group. Finally, advertising practitioners' perceived effectiveness of older models by product category is lower if the intended audience was general in comparison to an intended audience of older consumers, regardless of model age. This is confirmed by paired-sample t-tests between the target groups older people and general audience by model age group (all significant at the 1%-level [not shown]).

Discussion

Attitudes in terms of communication objectives and effectiveness of older spokespersons

Our survey indicates that advertising practitioners in Japan have positive – or at least not negative – attitudes about older spokespersons in terms of their communication objectives and effectiveness (see also Kohlbacher, Prieler et al., 2011b). The highest score was given to the item "Mood with older spokespersons aids persuasion" and the second highest to "Older spokespersons help enhance source credibility" for both model age groups. This result is in line with the findings by Greco (1988), and the second is especially in line with research results from experimental studies on the effectiveness of older models in advertising (Bristol, 1996; Milliman & Erffmeyer, 1990). Indeed, a field experiment conducted by Bristol (1996) revealed that younger endorsers were perceived to be less credible than middle-aged and older ones, and Milliman and Erffmeyer's (1990) research on older consumers' reactions to models of different ages (young, middle, and old) in advertising showed that while credibility scores were significantly affected by model age, favorability scores were not. Older consumers' favorability scores did not differ significantly for models of the three age groups, but they considered middle-aged and older models significantly more credible than young models shown in identical advertisements (Milliman & Erffmeyer, 1990).

It is interesting to note that the Japanese advertising practitioners thought that the 65+ model age group is more effective in aiding persuasion through mood and that it enhances source credibility even further than the 50–64 age group, even though the latter is only a non-significant tendency. Maybe advertising practitioners share the opinions of Bristol (1996) who argues that the perceptions of lack of credibility of a younger endorser may reflect a belief in the "inexperience of youth" and that older people may also lack trust in the opinions of the younger generation. Research has shown that consumers tend to judge the source credibility of advertisements on the basis of peripheral elements, such as physical characteristics and appearance (Guido, Peluso, & Moffa, 2011), and age obviously determines these quite strongly. Overall, these findings seem to be in line with the accepted theories of endorsement in advertising (McCracken, 1989; Tellis, 2004).

Finally, despite the positive tendencies and the fact that the attitudes were at least not negative, a careful interpretation of our findings should acknowledge that the advertising practitioners' perceptions of the effectiveness of older models are mixed. While approximately 40% (39.34% for 50–64 and 40.44% for 65+) of our respondents agreed that "Older spokespersons are effective at gaining comprehension," only roughly one-third (32.97% for 50–64 and 33.51% for 65+) agreed that "Older spokespersons are effective for gaining intention to purchase," and only approximately 20% (20.54 for 50–64 and 22.28% for 65+) agreed that "Older spokespersons are effective for gaining purchase." Previous research also shows mixed results in connection with the effectiveness of older models (Greco & Johnson, 1997; Greco & Swayne, 1992; Greco, Swayne, & Johnson, 1997; Klock & Traylor, 1983), and it seems that it depends on a variety of variables, such as product or service type, communication objectives, and the conspicuousness of its consumption. But it may be safe to say that it is more important for the model's age to fit the product's age-orientation for younger consumers than for older ones. Indeed, Greco (1997) for instance claimed that the majority of research evidence indicates this. This may be the reason why our respondents have not been able to provide a clear verdict on many of the statements that they were confronted with.

In addition to asking about the attitudes toward older spokespersons and models, we have also assessed the Japanese advertisers' attitudes toward older people in general by using the Japanese version of Palmore's (1998) Facts on Aging Quiz. Our respondents on average only achieved a 50.1% rate of correct answers, which is surprisingly low in comparison to other Japanese media professionals; Enda and associates (2007) surveyed Japanese broadcasters and their overall rate of correct answers was 70.6%. This difference can partly be explained by the fact that we used a version of the Quiz that included a "don't know" option. While only 50.07% of the answers were correct on average, only 18.96% were wrong and 29.69% were "don't know" answers. But this still means that 48.65% of the answers were not correct. This shows that advertising practitioners know comparatively little about older people. Taken together, these findings about Japanese advertising practitioners' attitudes toward older spokespersons/models and older people in general also seem to be in line with content analytic research on Japanese television advertisements showing that older people are clearly underrepresented (Hagiwara et al., 2009; Prieler et al., 2011a; Yamanaka, 2000).

General views on older models in advertising

The intention to use (more) older models exists, even though it is not very strongly pronounced. This intention is not given when the target is a general audience, though. This may have to do with the perceived risks and problems of using older models. Indeed, a higher percentage of respondents argue for more pre-testing with older models than with younger ones and even more so for the age group 65+ than for the age group 50–64. Even though more respondents disagreed than agreed with the statement "There are greater risks of negative effects on a general audience when older spokespersons are used," still more than 20% and almost 25% for younger old models and older old models respectively agreed with the statement.

These perceived risks of using older people and especially for using them when targeting a general audience may stem from an assumed low attractiveness attached to older models. Mazis and associates' (1992) review of the literature and their subsequent empirical study revealed, for example, a consistently negative linear relationship between model age and model attractiveness, that is, older models are viewed as less attractive. This is important, as empirical evidence shows the importance of attractiveness and other spokesperson characteristics for advertisement and product evaluations (Petroshius & Crocker, 1989) and the potential negative effects of consumers' comparisons with models in advertisements (Richins, 1991). Similarly, the theory of social comparison processes and the resulting principle of similarity or congruence between advertising cues and intended audience and their self-concept also support the argument for using similar models to the target group (Day & Stafford, 1997; Festinger, 1954; Hoffmann et al., 2012; Hong & Zinkhan, 1995), and advertising practitioners may be well aware of this. Therefore, the use of "cognitive-age congruent" models or spokespersons has been argued as proving fertile as a consumer's self-perceived age interacts with the perceived age of the model or spokesperson seen in an advertisement, and can subsequently influence the response to the advertising message (Chang, 2008; Van Auken & Barry, 2009). This may be one more reason why advertising practitioners are somewhat reluctant to use older models. Indeed, research has shown that – similar to other nations – older Japanese consumers' cognitive age tends to be lower than their real (biological) age (Kohlbacher & Chéron, 2012; Sudbury-Riley et al., 2015; Van Auken, Barry, & Bagozzi, 2006). Our qualitative interviews and the pre-test also confirm this perception among advertising practitioners.

A high percentage (43%) of our respondents supports the idea that older models in television advertisements serve as a role model for the older audience. A smaller percentage agrees that older people actually learn behavior from these portrayals. This is different from Greco's (1988) research where most of the respondents did not think that older consumers learn how to behave from the portrayals of older models in advertising or that they serve as role models for older audiences. Implicit in the responses to these statements may be a view that if older consumers are learning from older models, then these models must be effective in terms of achieving communication objectives.

Finally, the fact that the majority agrees that there will be an increased interest by clients in using older models and an increase in the amount of older models during the next five years underlines the importance of research on older models in advertising. But it is yet to be seen if advertising practitioners will actually change their usage of older models in the future.

On the whole, our results for both the communication objectives and effectiveness as well as the general views are more or less in line with Greco's (1988), while Szmigin and Carrigan (2000a) found more negative opinions. However, a direct comparison has to be interpreted cautiously, given that these studies were conducted many years ago in different countries and business environments.

Factors influencing the intention to use more older models

There seem to be two factors that are having a particularly strong, positive impact on the intention to use (more) older models: "Perceived effectiveness of older spokespersons" and "Expected increase in older models in the future," which is strongly connected with the expected client interest in using more older models. Against this background the first factor can be seen as an internal one (influenced by the advertising manager's or creative's own perceptions and experience) and the second as an external one (influenced by other agencies and clients). The impact of the internal factor is stronger than that of the external one.

"Perceived socialization effects of older models" and "Perceived risks and problems of using older models" do not play such an important role after all. This shows that even though advertising practitioners know about the risks of using older models, it does not necessarily affect their intention to use them. Finally, given that the variance explained is 19 and 23% respectively, there are obviously also additional factors at play. Further research is needed to identify these.

Product categories and match-up hypothesis

The results that advertising practitioners find older spokespersons effective for the product categories health-related products and finance/insurance is in line with content analytic research on Japanese television advertisements (Hagiwara et al., 2009; Prieler et al., 2009b, 2011a; Yamanaka, 2000) and also with the surveys by Greco (1988, 1989) in the United States and Szmigin and Carrigan (2000a) in the United Kingdom. It is interesting to note that the former holds true for the case of an older target group, while the latter holds true for a general audience. This is a new insight beyond what we know from content analyses which usually only analyze the older models and rarely distinguish between target groups of advertisements (Greco, 1988).

Previous research on consumer reactions to older models may offer some explanation here, for example, Rotfeld and associates' (1982) finding that youth-oriented products are best with young models and older-oriented products are best with older models. Our findings seem to underline this as they show that advertising practitioners' perceived effectiveness of older models are higher for age-oriented product categories than for youth-oriented product categories. In a similar vein, Day and Stafford (1997) concluded that older models in advertising can become a dissociative reference group in certain circumstances jeopardizing young adult patronage of certain services. Indeed, research has shown the impact of the source credibility on purchase intention to rise with increasing consistency between the endorser's physiognomy and the advertised product (Guido et al., 2011). The same is true of the similarity or congruity between the audience and the advertisement model or spokesperson (Hoffmann et al., 2012; Oakes & North, 2011). Overall, our findings seem to suggest that the match-up hypothesis is well at work with advertising practitioners in Japan.

Furthermore, it seems that Japanese advertising practitioners find older spokespersons most effective when the advertised product is targeted at older consumers and when the older spokesperson is in the 50–64 age group rather than the 65+ age group. This latter finding is in line with the observation by Hagiwara and associates (2009) and Prieler and associates (2009b) that in Japanese television advertisements the age group 65+ is clearly underrepresented while this is not the case for the age group 50–64. According to Mazis and associates (1992), the "use of young models could be judged as an effective strategy for cultivating younger as well as older markets" (p. 35), which may be one reason for the observed underrepresentation of older people. At the same time, the use of older models, which would be perceived as reasonably attractive to an older audience, could be seen as consistent with a strategy designed to stimulate selective demand among aging market segments (Mazis et al., 1992). Further research to confirm this is needed.

Implications

Previous research and our own results suggest that choosing the right models and portraying them appropriately are crucial but difficult tasks in marketing management and advertising creation. Advertisers need to carefully evaluate each situation individually and make a decision based on thorough research and a variety of different variables and influencing factors in order not to alienate either younger or older consumers.

There are six main implications from our research: 1) Overall, older spokespersons may be effective in achieving communications objectives depending on the purposes, product category, and target group. 2) Older spokespersons may be particularly effective in aiding persuasion through mood and in enhancing source credibility. 3) The interest by companies to use older models in advertising is going to increase over the next years and so will the number of older models. 4a) When targeting an older audience, older spokespersons may be particularly effective for the product category of health-related products; when targeting a general audience the product category is financial services/insurance. 4b) Regardless of the target audience, older models are more effective for age-oriented product categories in comparison to youth-oriented ones. 5) Regardless of the product group, older spokespersons may be more effective when targeting an older audience than a general audience and when they are aged 50–64 than when they are aged 65 and older. 6) The intention to use (more) older models in advertising is positively affected by the perceived effectiveness of older spokespersons and the expected increase in older models/expected client interest in the use of older models.

These implications are not only important for domestic businesses in Japan, but also of interest to marketers and advertisers from other countries who want to target the Japanese market. Given that Japan is the world's most aged society, experts have pointed to the fact that managers and marketers around the globe can learn from experimenting in the Japanese "lead market" and, indeed, some foreign companies have already invested to take advantage of attractive opportunities represented by the demographic trend in Japan (Kohlbacher, Gudorf et al., 2011; Kohlbacher & Rabe, 2015). Our findings may thus help both domestic as well as foreign businesses in making decisions pertaining to targeting this attractive market segment in Japan. Moreover, the findings from Japan may also prove useful to both Japanese and foreign companies who want to develop the growing older people's market in other countries as well, as more and more countries experience the demographic shift around the globe. This may eventually even lead to a global consumer culture of older people with associated global consumer culture position strategies emerging (cf. Okazaki et al., 2010).

Finally, according to Rotfeld (1982), the reasons for greater use of older models in advertising are twofold: First, in terms of communication strategy, the inclusion of older models might improve the advertising appeal directly or collaterally aimed at older consumers. Second, there is the critical "social responsibility" as well as ageism concern that more visible and positive use of older people in advertising could assist in providing some much needed improvements in our cultural perspectives on the old and aging (Carrigan & Szmigin, 1999, 2000b; Hagiwara et al., 2009; Horiuchi, Shibata, Watanabe, & Haga, 2010; Rotfeld et al., 1982). This chapter has tried to shed some light on the current situation and circumstances of using older people in advertising in the world's most aged society, Japan. In addition to new insights, there are interesting similarities and dissimilarities to previous research conducted in the United States and United Kingdom several years ago.

5
Consumer Response to the Portrayal of Older People in Television Advertising

This chapter aims to contribute to the state-of-the-field of research on older consumers and advertising in general and the Japanese older consumer in particular. It focuses on the advertising usage and consumer response to the portrayal of older people in television advertising based on a large sample survey conducted in Japan. Our empirical study is the first one to analyze the response of older Japanese consumers to the portrayal of older people in television advertising. We investigate the level of ad usage in making purchasing decisions and the attitude and response toward advertising and the portrayal of older people therein.

Given the rising importance of the older market segment, the relevance of advertising in older consumers' purchasing decisions, and the issues related to the representation and portrayal of older people in advertising, it is surprising that empirical research on the consumer response to the portrayal of older people by advertising practitioners is scarce and that there are hardly any recent empirical studies available. The fact that research has revealed that older viewers are concerned about the lack of representation and the stereotypes of older people on television (e.g., Healey & Ross, 2002) and that there is a negative influence of mass media interactions on older consumers' orientations toward age-based marketing stimuli (Moschis et al., 1993) makes this issue even more pressing for marketers and advertising practitioners. However, those studies that do exist on consumer response portrayal of older people by advertising practitioners have mostly been conducted about 25 to 30 years ago (e.g., Festervand & Lumpkin, 1985; Kolbe & Burnett,

1992; Langmeyer, 1984) and there is no single study available from Japan. This chapter thus fills an important gap in the literature (see also Hagiwara et al., 2010; Kohlbacher, Prieler et al., 2011a, 2011b).

Literature review

Sources of information for older people

Previous research has often reported a preference for the mass media, especially television, and information content among older people (Gunter, 1998; Nussbaum et al., 2000; J. D. Robinson et al., 2004). Older consumers are said to differ from their younger counterparts in terms of information sources they use (Bernhardt & Kinnear, 1976) and the scope and intensity of their information searches (Laroche et al., 2004). However, while some researchers have found informal sources of information (such as friends, family, and neighbors) to be important to older consumers (e.g., Klippel & Sweeney, 1974), others found that formal information sources (such as the mass media) are more important information providers (e.g., Phillips & Sternthal, 1977). In conclusion, empirical evidence as to which type of information source is more important is inconclusive. Overall, however, it is obvious that the mass media and advertising play an important role in informing purchasing decisions of older consumers (for a detailed overview, see Chapter 1 and Kohlbacher, Prieler et al., 2011a).

Consumer response to the portrayal of older people in television advertisements

One of the earliest empirical studies that included questions on the perception of the portrayal of older models in television advertising was Davis's (1971) survey of retired US Americans in 1969. While 44.6% of the respondents said that the image of older persons was presented factually and honestly on television, 48.7% were of the opinion that this was not the case for older persons in television advertisements (R. H. Davis, 1971). A replication of this study in 1982 revealed that while 59.2% of respondents felt the aged to be honestly and factually presented in television drama and 46.7% thought the same of older characters in comedies, only 39.7% felt the same for their depiction in television advertisements (R. H. Davis & Westbrook, 1985). In Schreiber and Boyd's (1980) US sample, the majority of the respondents reported older people in television advertisements to be either "active and healthy" or "likeable," while 31% noted that older people were not often shown in television advertisements (Schreiber & Boyd, 1980). Findings by Smith, Moschis, and Moore (1984) suggest that their older respondents feel that advertising practitioners do not portray older people in a positive or desirable manner, thus possibly alienating this audience. Langmeyer (1984) used five television advertisements as experimental stimuli on her sample of older adults to investigate their perceptions of older characters in television advertising. Her respondents did not find the portrayals to be offensive and they were not bothered by the underrepresentation of older people in television advertisements, even though they reported having become more sensitive toward the portrayal of older people than before (Langmeyer, 1984).

In yet another US sample of 271 usable responses, Festervand and Lumpkin (1985) found "pronounced disenchantment" expressed by their older respondents toward their portrayal in advertisements and a strong desire for a more positive portrayal of older models in advertisements in the future. They further showed that the negative portrayal of older characters in advertisements can influence attitudes toward a company and subsequent purchasing decisions (Festervand & Lumpkin, 1985). Indeed, the majority of the respondents indicated that they would discontinue to use a product if the advertisement promoting it was offensive, even though this would not mean that they necessarily also discontinued the use of other products from the same company; in addition, the probability of such boycott behavior is strongly reduced if the product offers attractive benefits (Festervand & Lumpkin, 1985). Overall, their findings indicate that older consumers generally do not have a positive attitude toward advertising, with the primary reason being a perceived lack of credibility and the inaccurate portrayal of older characters in advertisements (Festervand & Lumpkin, 1985).

In a replication and extension of Festervand and Lumpkin's (1985) study, Kolbe and Burnett (1992) examined the attitudes of young adults and older people by conducting a survey of college-aged and 65+-year-old respondents. Their results indicate that older people's and young adults' perceptions of the portrayal of older people in advertising did not differ significantly, while older respondents had a more negative view of advertising than young adults (Kolbe

& Burnett, 1992). Furthermore, negative portrayals of older characters in advertising adversely affected the older respondents' behavioral intent toward purchasing products, while young adults showed only little evidence of behavioral influence (Kolbe & Burnett, 1992). In contrast to Festervand and Lumpkin's (1985) sample, the older respondents in Kolbe and Burnett (1992) indicated that they would not purchase the product in case of negative portrayals even if it offered attractive benefits, thus showing a much stronger propensity to boycott. Finally, respondents agreed that advertisements that show older people in a negative light cause older viewers to have negative self-concepts and that they could not relate to older characters used in advertising (Kolbe & Burnett, 1992).

Using a national US sample, Moschis (1994) also found that more older respondents (31.4%) than younger ones (25.8%) agreed that they have avoided buying products because their advertisements were improperly stereotyping younger or older people. His evidence also indicated that the percentage of those taking offense at age stereotypes was especially high among a cluster identified as "healthy indulgers," that is, a particularly attractive segment of the market for older people which Moschis named "mature market" (Moschis, 1994). In the qualitative part of another study, Moschis and Mathur (2006) found that most of their respondents expressed at least some displeasure or unhappiness with advertisements that use older models or spokespersons. Even though the reason for this was not always very clearly articulated, the sensitivity to the stereotypical depiction of older people in advertising seemed to elicit strong (negative) emotions (Moschis & Mathur, 2006).

In a study on magazine advertisements by Robinson and associates (2003), 61.5% of the older respondents said that they would stop buying advertised brands because of the stereotypes in those brand advertisements. Older people were most offended by advertisements that portrayed them as being out of touch, unattractive, and objects of ridicule, while other advertisements that presented older people in a favorable manner were inoffensive and those that showed them as clever, vibrant, and having a sense of humor were even liked (T. Robinson et al., 2008; T. Robinson et al., 2003).

Last but not least, Ylänne and Williams's (2009) qualitative approach using focus groups revealed mixed results in terms of the reactions of their participants to older models in UK television advertisements.

Finally, it is important to note that how people perceive others of their age in advertising and the media in general also depends on how they think about their own aging as well as about older age in general (Bradley & Longino Jr., 2001). Depending on their prior preoccupations and emotional state, negative portrayals can have negative or positive effects and so can positive portrayals (Mares & Cantor, 1992). Besides first- and third-person effects have also been reported (T. Robinson & Umphrey, 2006) – in other words, if people believe that advertisements have a greater effect on others or themselves (Davison, 1983; Innes & Zeitz, 1988). Overall, it seems obvious that older consumers are aware of unfavorable depictions of older people in advertising and often hold a negative attitude toward this kind of portrayal. This negative attitude can even lead to product or company boycotts, with varying degrees of intensity.

Based on these previous findings, we were interested to see how and if older consumers use advertisements as a source of information, what their attitude toward the portrayal of older people in advertisements is (also differentiating between the 50–64 and the 65+ age group), and if perceived negative portrayals lead to the intention not to purchase a product.

Results

The results of this study are based on a survey for which we contracted Cross Marketing, a Japanese professional marketing research company experienced in academic research, to carry it out. A total of 1,834 fully completed questionnaires (no missing values) were obtained within less than 24 hours on November 28, 2009. Respondents came from all 47 prefectures across Japan and were aged between 20 and 79 (M=48.74, SD=15.599). For the analyses in this chapter, we mostly relied, however, on the older sub-sample of all respondents aged 50+ (N=911, M=62.27 years, SD=8.063). We split the 911 respondents aged 50+ among the two age groups: 50–64 (N=567, M=56.89 years, SD=4.499) and 65+ (N=344, M=71.15 years, SD=3.468). For further details about the method and sample, see Appendix 3.

First, we analyzed the ad usage of older consumers. Table 5.1 summarizes the responses to the items of the scale measuring the extent to which a consumer reports consulting advertisements before making purchase decisions in order to make better decisions.

Table 5.1 Ad use by age group

Statements	50-64				65+				
	N	% DA/SDA	% AG/SAG	Mean	Stdv	N	% DA/SDA	% AG/SAG	Mean	Stdv
To make sure I buy the right product or brand, I often look at advertisements to see what others are buying and using.	567	45.50	19.22	2.65	0.95	344	49.13	13.08	2.52	0.91
If I have little experience with a product, I often check with advertisements.	567	19.75	49.91	3.30	0.91	344	26.16	42.15	3.13	0.95
I often consult advertisements to help choose the best alternative available from a product class.	567	18.17	50.62	3.34	0.87	344	21.80	41.28	3.21	0.90
I often gather information from advertisements about products before I buy.	567	17.81	54.85	3.40	0.90	344	23.84	47.38	3.24	0.98
Summated Scale Total Cronbach's Alpha = .816	567	–	–	3.17	0.72	344	–	–	3.02	0.76

Note: Based on five-point scale from strongly disagree (1) to strongly agree (5). DA/SGA=Disagree/Strongly Disagree; AG/SAG=Agree/Strongly Agree. General means and standard deviations (Stdv) for the two age groups are also shown.

Except for the first item, both the percentages and the means suggest that most respondents consult advertisements to obtain information before making purchase decisions. A one-sample t-test reveals that the mean of the summated scale for the overall 50+ sample (M=3.12) is significantly different from the mid-point of 3 of the Likert scale (t(910)=4.75, p<.001). The same is true for the 50–64 age group (t(566)=5.68, p<.001), but not for the 65+ age group (t(343)=0.603, p=.547).

Comparing the responses from the age group 50–64 and 65+, we find that the means and the percentages for the agreement are lower for the 65+ age group than for the 50–64 one. A t-test confirmed these differences to be statistically significant for all items as well as for the summated scale (t(909)=2.927, p<.01, for the summated scale).

To analyze if there is a correlation between the age of older consumers and their general use of advertisements as a source of purchase-related information, correlations were calculated between the individual items, the summated scale, and the continuous age variable. All correlations are statistically significant, but rather weak (r=−.089, p<.001, 1-tailed, for the summated scale). Given that the correlations are negative, it seems that ad use decreases with higher age.

We also checked for gender differences in ad usage within each age group but found none (50–64: t(565)=1.179, p=.239; 65+: t(342)=−1.563, p=.119). For the 50–64 years age group, we found differences in ad usage by level of education (H(4)=12.752, p<.05), with a tendency to a negative relationship between level of education and ad usage (r=−.102, p<.05). For the 65+ age group, no differences by education level were found (H(4)=1.851, p=.763).

In the following we analyzed the attitude toward the portrayal of older people in television advertisements (Tables 5.2 and 5.3). The responses to the perceived stereotypical/inaccurate portrayal scale show that respondents feel that older people are portrayed inaccurately or in a stereotypical way in television advertisements, and future advertisements should portray them in a more positive manner (one-sample t-tests for the difference of the scale mean from the mid-point of 3: 50–64 group: t(566)=21.633, p<.001; 65+ group: t(343)=20.152, p<.001). Differences between the age groups 50–64 and 65+ are small, albeit statistically significant for the summated

Table 5.2 Perceived stereotypical/inaccurate portrayal

Statements	50–64						65+					
	N	% DA/ SDA	% AG/ SAG	Mean	Stdv		N	% DA/ SDA	% AG/ SAG	Mean	Stdv	
TV ads which I see do not show older people as they really are.	567	11.46	46.38	3.40	0.78		344	8.14	43.90	3.42	0.76	
I feel that future advertisements should portray older people in a more positive manner.	567	6.00	29.10	3.25	0.63		344	5.23	42.73	3.40	0.65	
I believe that how older people are portrayed in advertising merely reflects the general attitude of that company toward older people's place in society.	567	9.52	44.97	3.40	0.75		344	6.40	45.64	3.47	0.74	
Stereotyping of older characters occurs in advertising.	567	12.17	34.92	3.24	0.74		344	9.88	34.59	3.29	0.71	
In general, most TV advertisements in which older people appear are for medicines and health-related products.	567	5.29	74.78	3.87	0.80		344	3.78	77.33	3.97	0.76	
Summated Scale Total Cronbach's Alpha = .643	567	–	–	3.43	0.48		344	–	–	3.51	0.47	

Note: Based on five-point scale from strongly disagree (1) to strongly agree (5). DA/SGA=Disagree/Strongly Disagree; AG/SAG=Agree/Strongly Agree. General means and standard deviations (Stdv) for the two age groups are also shown.

scale, however with a very small effect size (t(909)=-2.366, p<.05). Gender differences were only found for the age group 50–64 years (t(565)=2.721,, p<.01), indicating that women perceived stereotyp- ical/inaccurate portrayal more strongly than men. Educational differ- ences were only found for the age group 65+ (H(4)=11.674, p<.05), with a slightly positive correlation (r=.153, p<.01), indicating that respondents with higher levels of education had a stronger propen- sity to perceive the portrayal as stereotypical/inaccurate.

Responses to the perceived negative portrayal scale are rather mixed (see Table 5.3). One-sample t-tests for the difference of the scale mean from the mid-point of 3 show that the mean for the 50–64 group is smaller (t(566)=−6.603, p<.001), but the difference of 0.02 for the 65+ group is not statistically significant (t(343)=−.607, p=.544). The differences between the two age groups is significant for the summated scale (t(909)=−3.517, p<.001); bivariate correlations suggest a positive relationship between age and the perceived nega- tive portrayal of older people in television advertisements (r=.151, p<.001). No significant gender or education differences within either of the two age groups were found for this scale.

Subsequently, we analyzed the intention not to purchase an adver- tised product in case the portrayal of older people in the adver- tisement is perceived as negative. Table 5.4 shows the responses to the purchase-intention scale. We found that respondents have the intention not to purchase a product if the portrayal of older people in the advertisement for this product is perceived as negative (one- sample t-test for the summated scale mean against the test value of 3; 50–64 age group: t(566)=9.123, p<.001; 65+ age group: t(343)=8.975, p<.001). The difference between the two age groups was found to be not statistically significant (t(909)=−1.222, p=.222). The bivariate correlation between age and the scale is not significant either (r=.05, p=.130). Thus, we did not find a positive correlation between the age of the older consumers and the intention not to purchase a product if the portrayal in the advertisement for this product is perceived as negative. We did not find any gender differences within either of the two age groups for this scale. Differences for educational level were significant only for the age group 65+ (H(4)=14.636, p<.05), with a tendency for a positive relationship between the intention not to purchase and the educational level (r=.159, p<.01), indicating that respondents with higher levels of education tended to have a

Table 5.3 Perceived negative portrayal

Statements	50–64					65+				
	N	% DA/SDA	% AG/SAG	Mean	Stdv	N	% DA/SDA	% AG/SAG	Mean	Stdv
TV advertisements suggest that older people are financially dependent on others.	567	31.39	15.17	2.83	0.75	344	23.84	19.77	2.95	0.73
I believe that TV advertising in general treats older people as socially inactive and unproductive.	567	23.63	26.81	3.03	0.81	344	15.99	31.40	3.17	0.79
Many of the TV advertisements I see portray older people as being lonely.	567	35.98	15.17	2.76	0.78	344	25.29	24.13	2.99	0.79
TV advertisements in general suggest older people as physically limited.	567	24.87	31.92	3.06	0.86	344	20.35	33.43	3.14	0.82
Overall, I do not believe that the portrayal of older people in TV advertising is changing for the better.	567	21.69	11.99	2.90	0.65	344	20.35	13.95	2.96	0.66
I find the portrayal of older people in TV advertisements to be insulting.	567	48.68	8.47	2.52	0.79	344	41.28	13.08	2.68	0.79
Summated Scale Total *Cronbach's Alpha = .807*	567	–	–	2.85	0.54	344	–	–	2.98	0.56

Note: Based on five-point scale from strongly disagree (1) to strongly agree (5). DA/SDA=Disagree/Strongly Disagree; AG/SAG=Agree/Strongly Agree. General means and standard deviations (Stdv) for the two age groups are also shown.

Table 5.4 Intention not to purchase

Statements	50–64					65+				
	N	% DA/SDA	% AG/SAG	Mean	Stdv	N	% DA/SDA	% AG/SAG	Mean	Stdv
If a new product is introduced with advertisements that portray older people offensively, I would not buy the product even if it offered benefits I found attractive.	567	16.58	38.62	3.29	0.87	344	11.63	43.60	3.40	0.85
If a product or service I use adopts an advertising campaign which portrays older people offensively, I will discontinue using it.	567	15.34	30.86	3.20	0.80	344	15.99	30.23	3.20	0.84
If I see an offensive ad for a product, I will not continue to purchase other products from the same company, even if I am a user of those products.	567	14.29	40.56	3.33	0.87	344	10.47	41.57	3.40	0.82
Summated Scale Total Cronbach's Alpha = .776	567	–	–	3.27	0.71	344	–	–	3.33	0.68

Note: Based on five-point scale from strongly disagree (1) to strongly agree (5). DA/SGA=Disagree/Strongly Disagree; AG/SAG=Agree/Strongly Agree. General means and standard deviations (Stdv) for the two age groups are also shown.

higher propensity to boycott products in case of perceived negative portrayal of older people in the advertisements.

We then continued to analyze the relation between a negative perception of the portrayal of older people in advertisements and the intention not to purchase a product if the portrayal of older people in the advertisement for this product is perceived as negative. For the overall 50+ sample, the perceived stereotypical/inaccurate portrayal scale correlates positively with the purchase intention scale (N=911; r=.425, p<.001) and so does the perceived negative portrayal scale, even though to a lesser extent (N=911; r=.188, p<.001). In short, there is a positive correlation between a negative attitude toward the portrayal of older people in advertisements and the intention not to purchase a product if the portrayal of older people in advertisements for this product is perceived as negative. Splitting the sample into the two age groups of 50–64 and 65+, it becomes obvious that the correlations are slightly stronger for the older age group: perceived stereotypical/inaccurate portrayal scale correlates positively with the purchase-intention scale (50–64: N=567; r=.399, p<.001; 65+: N=344; r=.465, p<.001) and so does the perceived negative portrayal scale with the purchase intention scale (50–64: N=567; r=.167, p<.001; 65+: N=344; r=.216, p<.001).

Finally, we used a multiple regression to assess the ability of ad usage, perceived stereotypical/inaccurate portrayal, perceived negative portrayal, and three demographic variables (age, gender, education) to predict the level of intention not to purchase a product if the portrayal of older people in the advertisement for this product is perceived as negative. Table 5.5 summarizes the results from the multiple regression analysis. For the overall 50+ sample, the independent variables explained 19% of the variance in the intention not to purchase. Only education and perceived stereotypical/inaccurate portrayal were statistically significant, with the latter recording a higher beta value (β=.42, p<.001) than the former (β=.08, p<.05). Splitting the sample into the two age groups of 50–64 and 65+, we can see two major differences between them. First, the total variance explained by the model for the 65+ age group is higher than for the 50–64 years age group (R^2=.23 vs R^2=.17). Second, in the case of the 50–64 years age group, the only statistically significant predictor is perceived stereotypical/inaccurate portrayal (β=.41, p<.001),

Table 5.5 Multiple regression on the intention not to purchase

Multiple Regression	All (50+) N=911				50–64 N=567				65+ N=344			
Intention not to purchase a product if the portrayal of older people in the advertisement for this product is perceived as negative scale	B	SE B	β	p	B	SE B	β	p	B	SE B	β	p
Constant	0.72	0.25	–	0.00	0.62	0.45	–	0.17	1.25	0.71	–	0.08
Age	0.00	0.00	0.03	0.32	0.01	0.01	0.04	0.36	-0.01	0.01	-0.04	0.45
Gender	0.02	0.04	0.01	0.65	0.05	0.06	0.04	0.37	-0.04	0.07	-0.03	0.58
Education	0.05	0.02	0.08	0.02	0.04	0.03	0.05	0.23	0.08	0.03	0.13	0.01
Ad use	0.05	0.03	0.05	0.12	0.06	0.04	0.06	0.14	0.03	0.04	0.03	0.51
Perceived stereotypical/inaccurate portrayal of older people in TV ads	0.63	0.05	0.42	0.00	0.62	0.07	0.41	0.00	0.64	0.08	0.44	0.00
Perceived negative portrayal of older people in TV ads	-0.02	0.04	-0.02	0.64	-0.04	0.06	-0.03	0.47	0.01	0.07	0.01	0.82
R^2	0.19				0.17				0.23			

while for the 65+ age group both perceived stereotypical/inaccurate portrayal (β=.44, p<.001) and education are statistically significant (β=.13, p<.05).

Discussion

Our results indicate that while older consumers generally use mass media advertisements as a source of purchase-related informa-tion, there is at the same time a negative correlation between the age of consumers aged 50 and older and their general use of mass media advertisements as a source of purchase-related information. This finding of a negative correlation was not surprising, given the inconclusive nature of previous research on this matter as was outlined above and in Chapter 1. One explanation for the higher use of advertisements in making purchasing decisions among the 50–64 age group in comparison with the 65+ age group is that most of the former are still working, have a regular income, and are thus more strongly involved in regular consumption decisions, especially if they are still living together with their children. Indeed, within the 50–64 years age group in our sample, 31.7% report to be regular employees (65+ group: 4.9%), while 26.5% are full-time housewives (65+: 37.2%), and only 11.6% are not working at all (65+: 45.1%). Besides, 46.9% of the 50–64-year-olds in our sample are living in a two-generation household together with their children (or in some cases their parents), while the majority of our respondents in the 65+ age group are living in one-generation households (husband and wife). Another explanation might simply be that they prefer other purchase-related information sources, such as family and friends. It is also interesting to note that we did not find any gender differ-ences. Even though not perfectly conclusive, the tendency that ad use is lower for people with higher education levels seems to be in line with the literature (e.g., Moschis, 1987).

Analyzing the attitude toward the portrayal of older people in advertisements revealed that our respondents perceived the portrayal of older people in television advertisements as stereotyp-ical/inaccurate, but not necessarily as negative. The strength of this perception was positively correlated with age. It is obvious that older consumers in Japan are critical of the portrayal of older people in television advertisements, perceiving it to be at least stereotypical and inaccurate. While the perception of the portrayal is not necessarily negative, it is not positive either. Overall, our findings seem to be in line with previous research as outlined in the literature review above. Indeed, they seem to support Robinson and associates' (2003) observation that there seems to be a growing awareness and concern among older people about how they are portrayed in advertising.

Looking at the individual items of the perceived negative portrayal scale suggests that some of the statements, such as "I find the portrayal of older people in TV advertisements to be insulting," might have been too strong to receive full-fledged agreement from the respondents. Advertising might portray certain (groups of) people in a stereotypical way, but insulting them would not only be unethical but also harmful to business. Two statements that achieved means that were significantly higher than the midpoint of 3 were "I believe that TV advertising in general treats older people as socially inactive and unproductive" (t(910)=3.030, p<.05) and "TV advertisements in general suggest older people as physically limited" (t(910)=3.319, p<.001). This finding can probably be explained by the relatively high percentage of older models appearing in television advertisements for health-related and anti-aging products. The fact that the negative attitude toward the portrayal was stronger for the 65+ age group than for the 50–64 age group might stem from the fact that we had asked respondents about the portrayal of older people aged 65 and older and that the younger age group thus did not identify or bother to the same degree with this issue. The inconclusive findings regarding gender and education require further research into the negative attitudes toward the portrayal of older people in advertisements and their antecedents.

Our results further show that older consumers generally have the intention not to purchase a product if the portrayal of older people in the advertisement for this product is perceived as negative, a finding that confirms results from previous research (Festervand & Lumpkin, 1985; Kolbe & Burnett, 1992; Moschis, 1994; T. Robinson et al., 2003). However, a correlation between the age of the older consumers and the intention not to purchase was not supported by the data, lending support to the assumption that this issue is of equal importance to the 50–64-year-olds and their older counterparts.

This seemed to be the case regardless of gender, but educational level apparently influenced only the older 65+ cohort in their intention to boycott products whose advertisements portray older people negatively.

We found a positive correlation between a negative attitude toward the portrayal of older people in advertisements and the intention not to purchase a product if the portrayal of older people in the advertisement for this product is perceived as negative. This correlation did not show any significant differences when analyzed separately for the 50–64 age group and the 65+ age group. This probably means that regardless of the older age cohort people belong to, they are more likely to boycott a product because its advertisements stereotype older people or even portray them negatively if their attitude toward the portrayal of older people in advertising is already negative. This phenomenon seems also to hold true across differences in gender and educational levels.

Interestingly, the results from the regression analysis found only the perceived stereotypical/inaccurate portrayal, but not the perceived negative portrayal to significantly predict the intention not to purchase. One explanation for this might be the high number of respondents who did not clearly voice their opinion on the perceived negative portrayal by opting for the (neutral) mid-point. However, the need for further research to understand the differences and/or the relationship between perceived stereotypical/inaccurate portrayal and perceived negative portrayal is warranted. The finding that once more educational level only played a significant role for the 65+ age group could be a mixture of the fact that more educated people might be more critical toward advertising in general as well as the fact that the 65+ age group identifies with the represented images and so feels closer to it than the 50–64 age group. This merits further research as well.

Last but not least, we would like to emphasize that the issues that we have analyzed in this chapter are not limited to older consumers but are also relevant to younger consumers. In our study, younger consumers (20–49 years of age) also noticed the stereotypical and inaccurate portrayal of older people in television advertising, even though they agreed with the statements in the questionnaire to a lesser extent than the 50+ age group. And, more importantly, they as well indicated an intention to boycott products and/or companies if the portrayal of older people in the advertisement for this product is perceived as negative. Again, their agreement was lower than that of the 50+ group but still around 30% agreed that they may not make purchases in that case.

Implications

There are three main conclusions from our research: 1) Older consumers rely to a fair amount on advertising as an information source in making purchase decisions. 2) Older consumers perceive the portrayal of older people in Japanese television advertisements as stereotypical/inaccurate and partly negative even though not necessarily as insulting. 3) Older (and younger) Japanese consumers have the intention not to purchase a product if its advertising is perceived as portraying older people negatively, that is, they are willing to boycott these products and/or even the company (and its other products).

The practical implications of our findings are obvious: 1) Advertising is a good means to target and approach older consumers and inform and influence their purchasing decisions. 2) Advertisements should be created in a way that does not portray older people in a stereotypical/inaccurate or negative way and thus alienate or annoy older (and maybe even younger) consumers, eventually even leading to product or company boycotts. Given the results from content analyses of advertisements in Japan and other countries, it is surprising to see how careless or maybe unaware advertising practitioners are of these issues. Miller and associates (2004) have suggested that "one might expect that many of the images of the elderly in advertising would be a function of marketing strategies designed to meet the needs of increasingly affluent seniors" (p. 316) and Robinson and associates (2003) warn that "as marketers begin to discover the potential size and spending power of the senior market segment, they should take heed to how their advertising addresses senior citizens" (p. 516). Indeed, the finding of a negative influence of mass media interactions on older consumers' orientations toward age-based marketing stimuli has been explained by the stereotyped depiction of older people in mass media causing older people to react adversely to such depictions (Moschis et al., 1993). Therefore, the advertising industry should be as concerned about its social esteem as with its selling effectiveness because if it "fails to address their use of older negative stereotypes, they risk alienating the rapidly growing older market and dissuading younger consumers" (T. Robinson et al., 2008, p. 249). This seems to be especially true in the world's most aged society, Japan.

6
Conclusion and Outlook

Population aging is a powerful megatrend affecting many countries around the world. This demographic shift has vast effects on societies and economies as well as businesses and the advertising industry. In the preceding chapters we have presented findings from a comprehensive research project on advertising in the aging society of Japan. As explained, given that it is the most aged society in the world, Japan is particularly suitable for a study of the implications of population aging. Analyzing data from a large-scale content analysis and questionnaire surveys among advertising practitioners and consumers in Japan, our research shows that older people (especially women) are highly underrepresented and are generally portrayed in stereotypical, albeit not necessarily unfavorable, ways. This is despite the fact that advertising practitioners have a generally positive view toward using older models, even though only for an older target audience. Finally, both younger and older consumers perceive the representation of older people in advertising as stereotypical and partly negative and are willing to boycott companies portraying older people negatively.

Representation of older people

Our content analysis of around 3,000 television advertisements shows a strong underrepresentation of older people compared to demographic reality. This is even more pronounced for the 65+ age group and older women, which is in line with previous literature, and it seems older people, and particularly older women, are still not regarded as valuable enough to be shown in advertising. However, the study shows a few positive signs, such as an increase of older people in television advertisements between 1997 and 2007 (though with a high amount of celebrities), an increasing appearance alone and in major roles which might indicate their increased status in society, an increase of older people shown in the workplace (which shows them as active), and an increase of favorable depictions of older people.

These findings of our content analysis somehow reflect the mixed views of advertising practitioners in our survey. On the one hand, practitioners expect an increased interest by clients in using older models and an increase in the amount of older models in the future. In addition, their general views on older people in advertising in terms of communication objectives and their effectiveness are seen as positive (or at least not as negative), and older people seem to be especially useful for enhancing mood, persuasion, and credibility. On the other hand, older models are still regarded as only useful when targeting an older audience (versus a general audience), when older models are younger (50–64) and not older (65+), and for product categories older people are stereotypically associated with, such as the health/medical product category and financial services/insurance (which are often about health insurance or retirement funds). Such limited usage shows the perceived risk of using older people among advertising practitioners, especially for targeting the general audience.

Stereotypical portrayals and underrepresentations of older people are problematic, since consumers rely heavily on advertising as an information source in making purchase decisions. Consumers perceive the portrayal of older people in television advertisements as stereotypical/inaccurate and partly negative, albeit not necessarily as insulting. Not surprisingly, the older age group (65+) had an even stronger negative attitude toward the portrayal of older people than the 50–64 age group, probably because they identify more with people 65+ in the advertisements. What practitioners should note, however, is that consumers are even willing to boycott products and/or companies portraying older people negatively in their advertising. And this does not only apply to older consumers but also to younger consumers (20–49 years of age), even though to a lesser degree, with around 30% indicating this willingness.

Why are older people still ignored?

Our results that older people were still highly underrepresented and stereotyped in Japanese television advertisements is striking considering the aging society in Japan, the increasing role of older people in the marketplace, and the fact that practitioners seem to have a generally positive perception of them and that consumers even threaten to boycott products that negatively portray older people.

One reason for this perception might be that older people still do not have enough powerful support groups in Japan (Abrams et al., 2003), and Japanese advertising practitioners believe that Japanese people do not in fact have such positive images of older people as stated in previous literature (e.g., Palmore & Maeda, 1985). Another reason for such representations might be the use of the so-called "cognitive-age congruent" models – in other words, the response to an advertising message is most favorable to a model with which the consumer identifies (Chang, 2008; Van Auken & Barry, 2009). Research has shown that – similar to other nations – older Japanese consumers' cognitive age tends to be lower than their real (biological) age (Barak, 2009; Kohlbacher & Chéron, 2012; Moschis & Mathur, 2006; Stephens, 1991; Sudbury-Riley et al., 2015; Van Auken et al., 2006) and therefore they respond better to younger models than those of the same age as them (Bristol, 1996; Greco, 1989; Kohlbacher & Chéron, 2012). This might be one reason why advertising practitioners are reluctant to use older models.

Finally, advertising practitioners might believe that older models alienate younger consumers, as evidenced in our results that they generally want to use older models only when targeting older people. Previous research has indicated that the advertising industry is rather youthful in the United Kingdom and the United States (Greco, 1989; Szmigin & Carrigan, 2000a), and young people might not be able to imagine the world of older consumers (McCaughan, 2015; Nyren, 2007). While we have no data on the age profile of Japanese practitioners overall, our survey suggests that advertising practitioners know little about older people, as evidenced in the responses to Palmore's (1998) "Facts on Aging Quiz."

One big exception where advertising practitioners are seemingly comfortable with using older people is celebrities (see Chapters 2 and 3). In contrast to non-celebrities, celebrities are commonly used in Japanese television advertising for targeting any age group, since many celebrities are popular with multiple age groups, and being a celebrity seemingly trumps being an older person.

Social effects, ethical considerations, and outlook

Regardless of the reasons for the underrepresentation and stereotypical portrayal of older people in Japanese television advertising, such representations could lead to negative attitudes about older people (Gerbner et al., 1980; Haboush et al., 2012; Passuth & Cook, 1985) and to a negative self-image among older people, that is, feeling denied by society (Donlon et al., 2005; Gerbner et al., 1980; Mares & Cantor, 1992). Negative self-image and self-stereotypes might affect the well-being of older people (Garstka & Schmitt, 2004), even lead to hearing decline (Levy et al., 2006), and impair memory performance (Westerhof et al., 2010). In contrast, positive stereotypes and positive perceptions of aging could empower older people (Abrams et al., 2003), improve memory and health, increase longevity, and reduce cardiovascular stress (Levy, 1996; Levy, Hausdorff, Hencke, & Wei, 2000; Levy, Slade, & Kasl, 2002; Levy, Slade, Kunkel, & Kasl, 2002). However, these are not only issues for older people, since young people also internalize stereotypes, and these stereotypes become self-stereotypes with the same effects later in life (Levy, 2003).

Even advertising practitioners in our survey are aware of the situation that older models in television advertisements serve as role models for the older audience and might potentially influence the audience. Underrepresentations could, for example, lead to the situation that older people are only considered to be a small part of the population with little importance to society (Gerbner et al., 1980), even though the contrary is the case nowadays. In addition, stereotypes might be activated by the media, and older people tend then to behave in ways consistent with these stereotypes (Wheeler & Petty, 2001).

Underrepresentation is even more pronounced for older women. Their representation even decreased for the 65+ age group, which is in stark contrast to the reality that older women outnumber and outlive men in Japan. However, such a finding confirms the so-called double standard of aging (Sontag, 1972), in which society is more permissive of aging in men than in women. It also confirms negative attitudes toward older women in Japan (Formanek, 2008; Prieler et al., 2011a). Such representations perpetuate an unfortunate combination of ageism and sexism and communicate to and teach the audience that older women are not as valuable as older men and younger women in society (Bandura, 2009; Gerbner, 1998; Gerbner et al., 1980).

Given the results from our content analysis of advertisements and our consumer survey, it is surprising to see how careless or maybe unaware advertisers are of these issues. Advertising practitioners should be as concerned about their social esteem as with their selling effectiveness because using stereotypical representations risks alienating a rapidly growing consumer segment and potentially even younger consumers. The representation of older people has an influence on whether an audience likes an advertisement and the company image, and might even lead to consumers' intention for boycotting products (see Chapter 5; Festervand & Lumpkin, 1985; Kohlbacher, Prieler et al., 2011a; Kolbe & Burnett, 1992; Moschis et al., 1993; T. Robinson et al., 2008). Thus, advertisements should be created in a way that does not portray older people in a stereotypical/ inaccurate or negative way and thus alienate or annoy older (and maybe even younger) consumers, eventually even leading to product or company boycotts.

The implications of this discussion are not only relevant for Japan as the most aged society in the world, but also are of interest to advertising practitioners from other countries who want to advertise in Japan as well as for advertising practitioners in other countries who face similar demographic challenges. While results cannot be transferred 1:1 from one culture to another, Japan can be regarded as a "lead market" within all aging societies (Kohlbacher, Gudorf et al., 2011; Kohlbacher & Rabe, 2015).

However, beyond using older models as a communication strategy to target older consumers, advertising practitioners and companies also have a "social responsibility" for a more diverse, positive, and visible usage of older people in advertising to improve our cultural perspectives of older people and aging (Carrigan & Szmigin, 1999, 2000b; Rotfeld et al., 1982). While there have been guidelines on how to best portray older people for decades (R. H. Davis, 1980), such as presenting them in a variety of behaviors and showing them in a range of experiences, advertising has partly failed to address these issues appropriately. However, there are also some recent positive developments in other media which have increasingly also started to use alternative and more diverse images of aging (Richards, Warren, & Gott, 2012; Wallander, 2013) – something that is needed more in the future in all media, including advertising. If this does not happen soon, at a time when societies are aging around the world, one has to further think about public policies and regulating advertising (Carrigan & Szmigin, 2000a, 2000b; Perry & Wolburg, 2011). Advertisements could also play an important role in creating a positive image of aging.

Finally, corporate social responsibility also makes business sense. Kohlbacher and Weihrauch (2009) convincingly argue that given the right business model, socially and ethically responsible action can also yield economically responsible profits, not to mention positive reputational effects. Kohlbacher (2013) even went as far as saying that corporations do have a social – and fiduciary responsibility to develop and provide products and services for older people.

In an advertising context, this can also be explained by the audience-as-commodity model (Smythe, 1977; Webster & Phalen, 1997), in which audiences are seen as products, and advertisers are consumers of that audience product. That is, advertisers – as consumers – seek audiences that provide them with the greatest utility at the lowest cost relative to other options and given their budget constraints (Coffey, 2013; Hoskins et al., 2004). This utility or audience value depends on the unique, differentiable traits of each audience (Coffey, 2013), and, given the audience size and income of older people in Japan, their audience value is obviously high, which makes them an attractive target segment for advertisers. Thus, not only should the media please older people with their programs in order to attract them as audiences, but also advertising practitioners and advertisements themselves should create a positive relationship with older people, for example, through portraying them in a positive way.

Limitations and future research

Finally, we should mention the limitations of this research as well as avenues for future research. In the content analysis our definition of older people was 50 years or older for most variables, which might lead to different results than a definition of 65 years or older. Our consumer survey only highlighted the data from respondents aged 50 and older for the analysis. For a better understanding of the perceptions of the portrayal of older people in Japanese advertising and its consequences, further comparisons with younger age groups certainly merit consideration. Besides, in order to fully disentangle age, period, and cohort effects, cohort analysis based on a longitudinal research design would have been necessary (Rentz, Reynolds, & Stout, 1983).

Another limitation was our samples. Although we gathered a random sample from two different years in an attempt to cover a period of ten years, we can only claim representation for these two years. It would certainly also be interesting to know how the data develops in another ten years. For the consumer survey, our online sample might also be a limitation. Despite the fact that online research methods have become more and more reliable and accepted, our sample cannot be seen as fully representative of the Japanese population and thus does not allow for generalizations beyond the sampling frame of where it came from.

While we found an increase of older people in major roles and a more favorable image of this age group in our content analysis, we also suggest conducting more qualitative investigations into the representation of older people to provide a more contextual analysis of the data. Similarly, more research on the fine-grained level will be necessary to find out in which cases and circumstances advertisers best select and utilize older models as general recommendations seem to be difficult to make.

Television advertisements are only one type of advertisement and part of a bigger media environment. Thus, analyzing and asking about only television advertisements may not be representative or comparable to other forms of advertising or media. So, one should also investigate whether representations in other forms of advertisements and programming are similar to or different from our findings. Similarly, surveys among producers and audiences of other media content would be of interest for comparative reasons.

In addition, content analysis can obviously only comment on the content itself and thus possible effects can only be assumed. Similarly, consumers can only give their opinions, as can advertising practitioners. Thus, another valuable methodological avenue for further research would be the employment of experimental designs using actual advertisements as stimuli as is often done in consumer response research (e.g., Garcia & Yang, 2006). Although some studies have been performed (e.g., Donlon et al., 2005; Mares & Cantor, 1992), further research is required to determine the effects of and responses to different representations of older people.

Further research might also consider a differentiation between the usage of everyday older models by gender and by whether these models are celebrities – the latter accounting for a high percentage in several countries, especially in East Asia (see Chapters 2 and 3).

Since we only studied consumers in a single country, we cannot make any cross-cultural inferences even though these may play a role in consumers' attitudes toward advertising (e.g., Cui, Chang, & Joy, 2008). Thus, while this study and its results are limited to a single country, the Japanese case shares many similarities with previous studies around the world. We have also found some particularities that point toward similarities in the representation of older people in other East Asian countries. Therefore, we suggest further research in the form of comparative studies on the representation of older people in neighboring countries in Asia and in other parts of the world.

Last but not least, as the word *aging* in aging society already suggests, we are living in times of a demographic transition, and the implications of population aging for societies and economies are part of a dynamic process. Due to cohort and period effects as well as various social and economic factors, older people of the future are likely to be different from those of today, just as these were different from generations before. In fact, those who will become older people by the middle of this century have already been born and will grow up in different circumstances from the current older generation. In terms of business implications, this might mean that "the current [older people's] market in Japan, as we know it, might just be a 'window of opportunity' that could soon close. It is therefore important to prepare today for the silver market of tomorrow and to leverage the demographic crisis as an opportunity" (Kohlbacher, 2011, p. 294).

Afterword

Chuck Nyren

A first thought for many before immersing themselves in *Advertising in the Aging Society* might be that the focus is narrow, the data only of interest to marketers and academics in Japan.

This certainly would have been my first thought had these studies been released a decade or so ago. Back then I was a brash, naive young 50-something copywriter, author, and consultant with revolutionary ideas, ready to change the advertising world. Together with a handful of likeminded middle-aged subversives, we pounded out books and blogs, lectured to skeptical audiences, were interviewed relentlessly by the press. My polemical contribution, *Advertising to Baby Boomers,*[1] was cited as a Classroom Resource by The Advertising Educational Foundation.[2]

What we lacked to back us up were rigorous academic studies. There were plenty of skewed surveys by marketing and media companies, but astute advertisers (and yours truly) had trouble with their research techniques, even though the conclusions were supporting what I and others had been preaching. In my consulting, speaking, and writing I eschewed much of this marketing fodder. I thought it suspect.

I wish we'd had something similar to *Advertising in the Aging Society* back then, focusing on the United States, with exacting standards and no hidden agenda. We tramped on without essential data.

I wasn't prepared for an international response to our evangelism. Why would business professionals in Europe, Asia, and elsewhere care about marketing to baby boomers and older groups? Except in the United Kingdom, where a 50+ marketing movement was brewing, I hadn't done my homework. In dozens and dozens of countries, older folks were relatively healthy, still employed, contributing to thriving economies, had more discretionary income than previous generations. So much for my myopic worldview.

During my international consulting in Europe and elsewhere, I always begin my presentations with a quote from American Political Scientist Seymour Lipset (1922–2006) culled from his book *American Exceptionalism*: "Those who know only one country, know no country."[3] Then I say to the participants, "Whatever I tell you today will be specific to the 50+ Market in the United States. I am not the Ugly American marching into your country and telling you what to do and how to do it. Much of what I'll say will not be relevant to you. What I hope *will* happen: As you watch and listen, every so often certain concepts, ideas, and practices will ring true – and you'll know that what I've just said is more than likely a universal truth about advertising to this demographic. You will then be able to fashion marketing campaigns with a finely-tuned mix of country-specific and universal values."

From my experiences hopping from country to country, I was surprised to be learning as much about *my* country as I was learning about other countries.

Michael Prieler and Florian Kohlbacher have consistently posed clear and effective questions. For years I've been wrestling with many of the queries and conclusions included in *Advertising in the Aging Society*. A few examples:

Using older models and spokespeople in advertisements has been a bewildering issue for years. We now know how consumers in Japan react to these advertising methods.

In the United States and England, most older women receive little respect as models or spokespeople. If they don't look 20 years younger than they are, they won't be considered. If they do look younger than their years, another decade or so will be swept away with the help of a ham-fisted airbrush artist:

Twiggy's Photoshopped Olay ads banned in England

Beauty company Olay debuted its Definity eye cream campaign depicting model Twiggy looking far younger, smoother, and firmer than her then 59 years should suggest. The '60s fashion star appeared virtually wrinkle-free in the ads and, since her baby-faced visage was selling anti-aging cream to older women, quite a few people – including bloggers, news outlets, and the British Parliament – grew quite disturbed.[4]

There's nothing wrong with being positive and aspirational – you just have to temper it with dollops of reality so your marketing won't be dismissed as pie-in-the-sky nonsense.

And there is the issue of trust:

The trend (*using older spokespeople*) is driven by the $2-trillion spending power of baby boomers – born between 1946 and 1964 – who make up 26% of the population. After all, what middle-aged woman wants to buy moisturizer from a model who's too young to order a martini?[5]

Authors Prieler and Kohlbacher also tackle product categories and underrepresentation. A tongue-in-cheek quote from my book you might consider:

Watching television commercials, you'd think that I haven't brushed my teeth, bought laundry soap, or taken a shower in almost twenty years. As for big-ticket items – well, those rabbit ears work just fine on my 19-inch color TV. They just require a nudge and a jiggle every now and then, that's all. And if I need a new needle for my phonograph, I just get in my '73 Pinto and head over to the Goodwill and, when no one is looking, twist one off a dusty old turntable and wedge it in the front pocket of my 30-year-old chinos.

We now know how older Japanese consumers react when targeted solely for age-related products. United States consumers feel the same way (a universal truth). From the *Boston Globe*, 2009:

Take one night last week, chosen at random, when NBC Nightly News aired 17 commercials during its 30-minute broadcast. Of those 17 spots, 12 were for (in order): Zyrtec, an over-the-counter allergy medication; Citrucel Fiber Supplement With Calcium;

Advil PM, a combination pain reliever and sleep aid; Transitions prescription eyeglass lenses ("healthy sight in every light"); Spiriva HandiHaler, for use by COPD (chronic obstructive pulmonary disease) sufferers; the cholesterol-lowering properties of Cheerios; Bayer aspirin and its heart-attack prevention benefits; Omnaris nasal spray, a prescription allergy medication; Just For Men hair coloring (let's help graying old Dad get a date!); Boniva, which helps reverse bone loss in postmenopausal women, most notably actress Sally Field; ThermaCare heat wraps, for relief of muscle and joint pain; and Pepcid Complete, a heartburn and acid reflux remedy.[6]

From a blog post of mine circa 2009:[7]

The Backlash: If every time someone over 50 sees a commercial targeting them and it's always for an age-related product or service, pretty soon their eyes will glaze over, they'll get itchy and grumpy.

The Real Issue: Marketing and advertising folks grasping the fact that boomers will be buying billions (trillions?) of dollars' worth of non-age-related products for the next 20-odd years. If you target this group for toothpaste, computers, clothes, food, nail polish, sporting equipment, toenail clippers – anything at all (almost) – and you do it with respect and finesse, they will appreciate and consider your product.

Dave McCaughan, former regional head of research (Asia) at McCann, penned a trenchant essay in the May/June 2015 issue of *Research World*:

Aging Asia... So let's start with what we all should know. When marketers talk about Asia, they usually make the mistake of talking youth.[8]

When marketers talk about just about anywhere, they usually make the mistake of "talking youth." It seems to be another universal truth, certainly true in the United States and many European countries. Marketing to youth exclusively has been a major theme in my writing and consulting since 2003. The pull-quote on the cover of *Advertising to Baby Boomers*, specifically about technology:

> It will be the Baby Boomers who will be the first to pick and choose, to ignore or be seduced by leading-edge technology marketing. There's a simple reason for this. We have the money to buy this stuff. Experts say we'll continue to have the money for at least the next twenty years. Write us off at your own peril.

I was far from the first to suggest a necessary shift away from the 18–35 demographic. In 1990, two prophetic books were released: *Age Wave* by Ken Dychtwald[9] and *Serving the Ageless Market: Strategies for Selling to the Fifty-Plus Market* by David B. Wolfe.[10] Many others followed, including *The Definitive Guide to Mature Advertising and Marketing* by Kevin Lavery,[11] *Marketing to Leading-Edge Baby Boomers* by Brent Green,[12] and *The 50 Plus Market* by Dick Stroud.[13]

More from Mr. McCaughan in *Research World Magazine*:

> Toru Shibata, former president of Johnson & Johnson Consumer in Japan and now EVP of Cocokara Fine inc., points out that marketing departments and their research partners across the region are remarkably under-equipped to come to grips with this aging dynamic. Shibtata-san observes, "The problem is that not enough people in marketing have 'senior experience.' Companies don't have people in the right age bracket."

This is another theme of mine, and has been for over a decade. From a chapter contributed to *The Silver Market Phenomenon*, edited by Florian Kohlbacher and Cornelius Herstatt:

> Today's advertising industry needs a minor revolution. Talented men and women in their 40s, 50s, and 60s must to be brought into the fold if you want to target the Silver Market. This includes copywriters, graphic artists, producers, video directors, and creative directors. If you plan on implementing a marketing strategy that includes Baby Boomers as a primary, secondary, or tertiary market, and you turn it over to only people in their 20s and 30s, you will forfeit the natural sensibilities required to generate vital campaigns.

You can analyze marketing fodder all day and night, read count-less books about marketing to Baby Boomers, attend advertising and marketing conventions around the world, and soak up every-thing all the experts have to say. But the bottom line is this: if the right people aren't in the right jobs, what happens is what happens in all arenas of business failure and mediocrity.

And the reverse is true. If you had a product or service for late teens and twenty-somethings, and you walked into your adver-tising agency and your creative team was made up of only people in their 50s and 60s – I would imagine that you would be very, very worried.[14]

Returning to my opening sentence: A first thought for many before immersing themselves in *Advertising in the Aging Society* might be that the focus is narrow, the data only of interest to marketers and academics in Japan.

Not true. This is a book that can be tucked under your arm and taken everywhere around the globe.

My advice to Japanese marketing academics and practitioners: read as much as you can about other countries, immerse yourselves in their research and advertising to the 50+ demographic, and the veri-ties contained in *Advertising in the Aging Society* will surface as if in bas relief.

This is another universal truth.

Chuck Nyren

Author of *Advertising to Baby Boomers*, Consultant, www.chuck-nyren.com

Notes

1. *Advertising to Baby Boomers*, Chuck Nyren, Ithaca, NY, Paramount Publishing, 2005.
2. Advertising Educational Foundation, AEF provides educational content to enrich the understanding of advertising and its role in culture, society, and the economy. www.aef.com
3. Lipset, Seymour Martin. American Exceptionalism. New York: W. W. Norton & Company, 1996.
4. *Yahoo Health*, www.yahoo.com/health, January 2010.
5. "Demand for Older Models Grows," Monica Corcoran, *Los Angeles Times*, July 2008.

6. "Use Only as Directed," Joseph P. Kahn, *Boston Globe*, April 6, 2009.
7. "Boomer Backlash II," www.advertisingtobabyboomers, September 2009.
8. "Aging Asia," Dave McCaughan, *Research World Magazine*, No. 52, May/June 2015.
9. *Age Wave: How The Most Important Trend Of Our Time Will Change Your Future*, Ken Dychtwald, Bantam, January, 1990.
10. *Serving the Ageless Market*, David B. Wolfe, Mcgraw-Hill, June 1990.
11. *The Definitive Guide to Mature Advertising and Marketing*, Kevin Lavery, Millennium ADMP Plc, 1998.
12. *Marketing to Leading-Edge Baby Boomers*, Brent Green, Paramount Publishing, 2004.
13. *The 50 Plus Market: Why the Future Is Age-Neutral When it Comes to Marketing and Branding Strategies*, Dick Stroud, Kogan Page, 2005.
14. *The Silver Market Phenomenon: Marketing and Innovation in the Aging Society*, (2nd ed.) Florian Kohlbacher, Cornelius Herstatt, Springer Press, 2011.

Appendix 1: Method of Content Analysis

Sample and coding

The sample for this research is drawn from a database of television advertisements from the company Video Research that includes all advertisements being broadcast for the first time on any given day in the Greater Tokyo Area on the five commercial television stations: TV Tokyo, TV Asahi, Fuji Television, TBS, and NTV. This means that the database contains no duplicates. In order to establish a representative sample, we have randomly chosen 28 days with an equal distribution of weekdays over one year (for both 1997 and 2007). This resulted in 1,495 unduplicated television advertisements in 1997 and 1,477 in 2007: 2,972 in total. Within these, the 1997 advertisements included 1,236 advertisements with people; the 2007 advertisements included 1,220 advertisements with people (see also Hagiwara et al., 2010; Hagiwara et al., 2009; Prieler, Kohlbacher, Hagiwara, & Arima, 2009a; Prieler et al., 2009b, 2010, 2011a, 2011b, 2015).

Two Japanese doctoral students (one male and one female) who were blind to the research questions undertook the coding of all television advertisements independently. Reliability coefficients, as measured by Cohen's kappa, ranged above .80 for most variables. Only the variables for the categories of image (.705 for 1997; .692 for 2007) and social interaction (.704 for 1997; .777 for 2007) had lower results. Hayes (2005) notes that an agreement of .700 is sufficient if reliability is corrected for chance, all coders code all units, and disagreements between the coders are resolved. Our coders took all of these steps. While our reliability for image was slightly lower in 2007, it was still above the recommended chance-corrected agreement of .600 by Neuendorf (2011). To establish a final data set, disagreements between the coders were settled through discussion.

Variables

We used variables from previous research (B.-K. Lee et al., 2006; Mastro & Stern, 2003; Roy & Harwood, 1997; Simcock & Sudbury, 2006) that seemed to be particularly useful for analyzing the representation of older people in Japanese television advertisements and further developed them in pilot studies (Prieler, 2008a; Prieler et al., 2009b).

Gender. Characters in the television advertisements were coded as male or female.

Age. A character's age was first estimated within the following categories: 1–14 years old, 15–34 years old, 35–49 years old, 50–64 years old, and 65 years and over. In a second step of analysis, the categories were collapsed into younger or older than 50 years, since the number of people 65 years or older was rather small. Infants were excluded from this study, since their gender could not always be determined. The age of characters was determined in three ways (Simcock & Sudbury, 2006): (1) The age of the character was known (half of all were celebrities), (2) a reference to the age of the character was given, (3) the physical appearance of the character (e.g., hair color, thinning of hair, wrinkles).

Role. Both major roles and minor roles were investigated. Major roles depict the most prominent characters in advertisements and commonly involve speaking parts and close-ups. People in minor roles are present longer than three seconds or appear several times, speak little or not at all, and support the major role. Advertisements including one older person in a major role and one older person in a minor role were coded as both. People in the background role were not examined for this study, since we reasoned that the faces of people in background roles are often unclear, making the coding of age problematic.

Celebrity. A celebrity is a person who is recognized in a society or culture. This does not necessarily mean that the coder remembers the name of the celebrity. People in minor roles and background roles were not examined for this study, since we reasoned that the faces of people in such roles are often unclear, making the coding of a celebrity problematic.

Image. The image of the older person in the television advertisement was coded in the following way: favorable, neither, or unfavorable (Simcock & Sudbury, 2006). A favorable portrayal was one where older models were shown as authoritative, competent, skillful or controlling, and/or enjoying a particular activity. An unfavorable portrayal was one where older models were shown as incompetent (comical or otherwise), helpless, a victim, weak, or displaying stereotypically negative behavior associated with age (e.g., bad temper, forgetfulness).

Social interaction. This variable investigates if older people are interacting with other people in advertisements. The social interactions of older people with other people were coded in the following way: alone, with older people, with adults (younger than 50), with a child, or with multiple generations. If several social interactions appeared, the most prominent one was coded.

Setting. The setting is the place where the older person appears in the advertisement. If there were several settings, the dominant setting was coded. The setting was coded from the perspective of the older person. For example, for a waiter in a restaurant serving food, the setting would be "workplace," but the setting would be "other indoors" for the person being served. We coded the following settings: home (inside), workplace (inside), other inside, outside, and other.

Product category. The product categories in this research, which are in accordance with the product categories commonly used in Japan, were provided by the database of television advertisements; these product categories were as follows: foods/beverages, service/leisure, cosmetics/toiletries, distribution/ retailing, pharmaceuticals/medical supplies, automobile/related products, real estate/housing, finance/insurance, household products, apparel/fashion/ accessories/personal items, precision instruments/office supplies, home electric appliances/AV equipment, publications, materials, and other.

Appendix 2: Method of Advertising Agency Survey

Sample

Our research questions were explored via a large sample survey of advertising practitioners (N=185) in Japan in July and August 2009 (see also: Kohlbacher, Prieler et al., 2011b; Kohlbacher et al., 2014). We used the online database of the widely read professional advertising magazine *Senden Kaigi* (www.sendenkaigi.com) in June 2009 to obtain the names and contact details of all advertising agencies with more than ten employees in the four main categories: 1) full service (487), 2) mass media (5), 3) in-house (8), and 4) foreign-owned (14). We focused only on agencies with more than ten employees, as smaller agencies are usually very specialized and their employees tend to be too busy to reply to academic research surveys. The selection of these four types of agencies was seen as consistent with our research objectives and previous research. Because we only had the addresses and phone numbers, but no names of individual people, we had a research assistant call each of the 514 advertising agencies individually, explain the purpose of our research, and ask for the company's participation in the survey. As an incentive, we included a hard copy of an article we had recently published in Japanese (Hagiwara et al., 2009).

For each of the 354 companies that accepted (68.9%), we asked for two people per agency – generally, the managers in charge of strategic planning and those in ad creation – to participate in the survey. In some agencies, especially smaller ones, one and the same person was responsible for both planning and creation, so, depending on the agency, we were given the names of one or two managers to whom we were to address the survey. A total of 433 questionnaires were sent out to the managers in July 2009. We received 185 returned questionnaires for an effective response rate of 42.7%. Table A.1 shows a brief description of our sample. Respondents ranged in age from 23 to 66 (M=46.87, SD=10.313); they were predominantly male (86.9%) and had an average of 21.28 years (Min=1, Max=44, Mdn=22) of work experience in the advertising industry.

Measures

The survey instrument was created in a series of steps following a systematic review of the literature. An original English version of the survey was prepared and subsequently translated into Japanese by one of the authors,

121

Table A.1   Description of the sample of advertising practitioners (N=185)

	%	n
Total Annual Revenue 2008 (USD)		
More than $1Bn.	3.2	6
Between $100 Mil. – $1Bn.	17.3	32
Between $10 Mil. – $100Mil.	51.4	95
Between $1 Mil. – $10 Mil.	23.2	43
Less than $1 Mil.	2.7	5
Missing	2.2	4
Number of Employees		
1,000 or more	1.6	3
500–999	2.2	4
300–499	7.0	13
100–299	18.4	34
50–99	23.8	44
10–49	44.9	83
1–9	2.2	4
Type of Advertising Agency		
Full service	82.7	153
Mass media agency	1.6	3
In-house agency	6.5	12
Other	9.2	17

and the translation was then carefully checked by three other bilingual senior researchers. A pre-test was conducted with managers in the older people's market divisions of the two largest Japanese advertising agencies (Dentsu and Hakuhodo) and managers at the research department of a large foreign agency's Japan office (McCann Erickson Japan). The feedback from the pre-test was intensively discussed and the questionnaire draft was amended accordingly.

Most of the questionnaire items and scales were adapted from Greco (1988, 1989) and the replication by Szmigin and Carrigan (2000a) and focused on the opinions of advertising practitioners about the communication objectives and effectiveness for older spokespersons, their general views on older models in advertising, and the effectiveness of older models by product category. As previously mentioned, one important contribution of our research is to distinguish between the younger and the older part of the older people's market. We therefore decided to ask each question twice: once defining older model/spokesperson as 50–64 and once as 65+. Going beyond the purely descriptive approach by Greco (1988, 1989) and Szmigin and Carrigan (2000a), we first factor analyzed the two question batteries about the communication objectives for older spokespersons (10 items) and about the general views on older models in advertising (13 items) using principal component analysis with varimax rotation. The resulting components were then subjected to a reliability analysis using Cronbach's alpha to create scales for further analysis. As for the battery about the communication objectives for older spokespersons, we ended up with a unidimensional scale consisting of eight items measuring the perceived effectiveness of older spokespersons. This scale had a Cronbach's alpha of .791 for the 50–64 age group and one of .833 for the 65+ age group. As for the battery about the general views on older models in advertising, we ended up with four two-item scales as follows: 1) intention to use older models (advocating the increased use of older models in the future), 2) expected increase in older models in the future (including an increased client interest in using older models), 3) perceived socialization effects of older models (on older viewers), and 4) perceived risks and problems of using older models (including negative effects on a general audience). The alphas were as follows: 1) .541/.550 (50–64 age group/65+ age group), 2) .886/.894, 3) .753/.730, and 4) .631/.646. Given the exploratory character of this research and the fact that the scales consisted only of two items each, these reliability values were deemed sufficient. This seems warranted since the effect of having a measure with lower reliability is to attenuate the correlation of that measure with other measures, thus reducing the statistical significance of tests. Therefore, any significant results using a scale with lower reliability are actually the product of a more conservative test of the hypothesis (e.g., Creyer & Ross Jr., 1997). Nevertheless, given the low reliability of the intention to use more older models scale and given that the question was very straightforward, we also repeated our multiple regression with the first question ("More older persons should be used in advertising") as a single-item measure as the dependent variable and were able to replicate our findings.

Finally, while Greco's (1988, 1989) and Szmigin and Carrigan's (2000a) list of product categories was compiled from research by Ursic and associates (1986), we created a new list based on content analytical research in Japan (Hagiwara et al., 2009; Prieler, 2008a), interviews with advertising agencies, and the pre-test to make sure our list suited the time and cultural context of the situation in Japan. Demographic data on the agency and the respondents was also requested.

Analysis strategy and techniques

To test and determine the views of advertising practitioners about the communication objectives and effectiveness of older spokespersons, their general views on older models in advertising, and the effectiveness of older models by product category, the percentages of those who agreed or strongly agreed with each attitudinal statement were compared to the percentages of those who disagreed or strongly disagreed (recommend or strongly recommend and not recommend or definitely not recommend in the case of the effectiveness of older models by product category), a practice also used by Greco

(1988, 1989) and Szmigin and Carrigan (2000a). One-sample t-tests were then conducted to check whether the means of the items differed significantly from the mid-point of three on the Likert scale or not. Paired sample t-tests were then employed to test if the attitudes and opinions differed depending on whether the older model/spokesperson was defined as 50–64 years of age or 65+, or depending on the target audience (older or general).

In order to evaluate which factors predict the intention to use older models, all scales were subjected to a multiple regression analysis with scale 1) as the dependent variable and scales 2), 3), 4), as well as the perceived effectiveness of older spokespersons scale as the independent variables. Preliminary analyses were conducted to ensure no violation of the assumptions of normality, linearity, multicollinearity, and homoscedasticity. Based on these analyses, a small number of outliers were removed from the analysis.

Appendix 3: Method of Consumer Survey

Sample

We contracted Cross Marketing, a Japanese professional marketing research company experienced in academic research, to carry out the survey (see also: Kohlbacher, Prieler et al., 2011a). The survey was conducted online using the company's regular consumer panel. Members of the panel were quota-sampled based on age and gender in accordance with their actual distribution in the Japanese population through a two-stage sampling process: 17,111 people were randomly selected from the company's panel and received a request to participate in the survey by email. Of these 3,210 accepted and filled in their demographic information for the screening process. A total of 1,834 fully completed questionnaires (no missing values) were obtained within less than 24 hours on November 28, 2009. Respondents came from all 47 prefectures across Japan and were aged between 20 and 79 (M=48.74, SD=15.599).

As the objective of this research was to replicate and extend previous research with the use of a different sample in a different country and to test for relationships between theory-driven concepts, we deemed such a quota sample appropriate, even though it does not necessarily enable us to make any population-related estimates or to generalize the findings to other populations. However, for such purposes, even convenience samples have been pronounced acceptable (e.g., Mathur & Moschis, 2005). Given that online surveys are becoming more and more common and accepted in marketing and communication research (Couper & Miller, 2008; Ilieva, Baron, & Healey, 2002) and that 91.1% of Japanese households were using the Internet in 2008 – including 84.9% of households with household heads aged 60 and older (Ministry of Internal Affairs and Communications, 2009) – conducting our survey online was deemed appropriate for the purpose of our research.

As this study deals with the response of older consumers to their portrayal in television advertisements, we only included data from respondents aged 50 and older. Fifty years of age as a cut-off point is in accordance with previous research on older consumers (e.g., Kohlbacher & Chéron, 2012; Moschis, 1994; Sudbury & Simcock, 2009b), and was judged appropriate for our purposes as well. The items on the portrayal of older people used the Japanese term *kōreisha* and defined it as 65 years and older as is common in Japan. However, we also wanted to measure the consumer response of the younger cohort in the older people's market aged 50–64 and this is why we included all respondents aged 50 and older in the data analysis for this chapter (N=911, M=62.27 years, SD=8.063). Table A.2 shows a description

Table A.2 Descriptions of sample of consumers by age group

		All (50+)		50–64		65+	
		N=	911	N=	567	N=	344
Variables		n	%	n	%	n	%
Gender	Male	437	48.0	274	48.3	163	47.4
	Female	474	52.0	293	51.7	181	52.6
Marital	Unmarried	59	6.5	52	9.2	7	2.0
Status	Married	743	81.6	472	83.2	271	78.8
	Separated/widowed	109	12.0	43	7.6	66	19.2
Household	No income	11	1.2	8	1.4	3	0.9
Income	< 3,990,000 JPY	319	35.0	165	29.1	154	44.8
	4,000,000–5,990,000 JPY	213	23.4	119	21.0	94	27.3
	6,000,000–7,990,000 JPY	142	15.6	106	18.7	36	10.5
	8,000,000–9,990,000 JPY	106	11.6	73	12.9	33	9.6
	10,000,000–11,990,000 JPY	49	5.4	38	6.7	11	3.2
	12,000,000–14,990,000 JPY	45	4.9	36	6.3	9	2.6
	15,000,000 JPY and more	26	2.9	22	3.9	4	1.2
Education	Junior high school	56	6.1	20	3.5	36	10.5
	Senior high school	393	43.1	223	39.3	170	49.4
	2-year-college, technical college	127	13.9	91	16.0	36	10.5
	College	311	34.1	216	38.1	95	27.6
	Graduate school	24	2.6	17	3.0	7	2.0
Household	1-person	92	10.1	50	8.8	42	12.2
Type	1-generation (husband-wife)	359	39.4	182	32.1	177	51.5
	2-generation (parent/s and child/ren)	361	39.6	266	46.9	95	27.6
	3-generation (parent/s, child/ren and grandchild/ren)	86	9.4	58	10.2	28	8.1
	Other (grandparent/s and grandchild/ren)	13	1.4	11	1.9	2	0.6
Occupation	Regular employee	197	21.6	180	31.7	17	4.9
	Contract/dispatched employee	35	3.8	34	6.0	1	0.3
	Part-time worker	87	9.5	68	12.0	19	5.5
	Full-time housewife	278	30.5	150	26.5	128	37.2
	Unemployed/not working	221	24.3	66	11.6	155	45.1
	Other	93	10.2	69	12.2	24	7.0

of our sample. We split the 911 respondents aged 50 and older among the two age groups: 50–64 (N=567, M=56.89 years, SD=4.499) and 65+ (N=344, M=71.15 years, SD=3.468).

The survey instrument was prepared in a series of steps following a systematic review of the literature. An original English version of the survey was prepared and subsequently translated into Japanese by two bilingual students. The translation was then carefully checked by the two authors and two additional bilingual senior researchers and a pre-test with 50 Japanese people of various age groups was conducted. The feedback from the pretest was intensively discussed and the questionnaire draft amended accordingly.

Measures

In order to measure the importance of advertising as an information source, we used a scale from Bush and associates (1999) which was meant to tap the social utility reasons for watching or reading advertisements. This scale consists of four, five-point Likert-type statements measuring the extent to which a consumer reports consulting advertisements before making purchase decisions in order to make better decisions. The scale used by Bush and associates (1999) was directly adapted from a scale by Bearden and associates (1989). Whereas the latter's scale had to do with one's tendency to seek information about products by observing others' behavior, the former's involves seeking information from advertising. Cronbach's alpha for the scale in our sample was .816 and thus deemed reliable. A principal component analysis of the four items showed that there was only one component extracted accounting for 64.6% of the variance, with all items loading highly on the component (all loadings > .7).

The attitudes of the respondents toward the portrayal of older people in television advertisements were measured using a five-point Likert-type scale ranging from strongly disagree (1) to strongly agree (5). A total of 15 statements dealing with the portrayal of older people in advertising were adapted from Festervand and Lumpkin (1985). Some of these items had also been employed by Langmeyer (1984) and Kolbe and Burnett (1992) and had originally been adapted from similar studies which examined women's attitudes toward advertising and role portrayals (Lundstrom & Sciglimpaglia, 1977; Sciglimpaglia, Lundstrom, & Vanier, 1979). The 15 items we adapted from Festervand and Lumpkin (1985), were items that had formed four different scales in their research: 1) negative portrayal – activities and financial, 2) negative portrayal – health and mental, 3) negative portrayal – negative toward company/product, and 4) negative portrayal – becoming more negative. Because Festervand and Lumpkin (1985) had obtained their scales through a factor analysis of a larger number of items and because of the assumption that our sample might differ significantly from theirs (more than 25 years have passed, different country/culture), we factor analyzed these 15 items in order to create scales that fit our sample. Principal component analyses were conducted on the 15 items with orthogonal rotation (varimax) and oblique rotation (direct oblimin). Both rotation approaches resulted in the same factor structure and because the assumption of correlated factors seems plausible, we report the results from the oblique rotation here. The Kaiser-Meyer-Olkin measure verified the sampling adequacy for the analysis, KMO = .866, and all KMO values for individual items were > .77, which is well above the acceptable limit of .5. Bartlett's test of sphericity, χ^2 (105) = 3501.88, p < .001, indicated that correlations between items were sufficiently large for PCA. An initial analysis was run to obtain eigenvalues for each component in the data and three components had eigenvalues over Kaiser's criterion of 1 and in combination explained 50.52% of the variance. One item was dropped from the analysis because its loadings on all of the three components were low (<.4). Repeating the PCA without this item confirmed the same component structure again.

Component 1 represents the actually perceived negative portrayal of older people in television advertisements, component 2 represents the perceived stereotypical/inaccurate portrayal of older people, and component 3 represents the intention not to purchase a product if the portrayal of older people in the advertisement for this product is perceived as negative. Summated scales were created for each component consisting of the individual items. 1) Perceived negative portrayal scale with six items and a Cronbachs's Alpha of .807, 2), the perceived stereotypical/inaccurate portrayal scale with five items and a Cronbachs's Alpha of .643 and 3), and the purchase intention scale with three items and Cronbachs's Alpha of .776. As expected, the three scales correlate with one another: 1) with 2): r=.4687; 1) with 3): r=.188; 2) with 3): r=.425, n=911, p < .001.

Education was measured as an ordinal variable on five levels ranging from low education (junior high school) to high education (graduate school; see Table A.2).

Analysis techniques

In order to identify the underlying dimensions represented in the attitudinal statements, principal component analyses were performed. To determine the ad use of the older consumers as well as their attitudes toward the portrayal of older people in advertisements, the percentages who agreed or strongly agreed to each attitudinal statement were compared to the percentages of those who disagreed or strongly disagreed, a practice also used by Festervand and Lumpkin (1985). We used both parametric and non-parametric tests to check for differences in the mean scores between age groups (t-tests) and educational levels (Kruskal-Wallis tests) and bivariate Pearson correlations to analyze the relation between the responses to the statements/scales and age of the respondents. We also used one-sample t-tests to test whether mean scores differ significantly from the mid-point of 3 on the Likert scales. Last but not least, multiple regression was used to assess the ability of ad usage, perceived stereotypical/inaccurate portrayal, perceived negative portrayal, and three demographic variables (age, gender, education) to predict the level of intention not to purchase a product if the portrayal of older people in the advertisement for the product is perceived as negative.

References

Abrams, J. R., Eveland, W. P. J., & Giles, H. (2003). The effects of television on group vitality: Can television empower nondominant groups? In P. J. Kalbfleisch (ed.), *Communication Yearbook 27* (pp. 193–219). Mahwah: Lawrence Erlbaum.

Aguirre-Rodriguez, A., Bosnjak, M., & Sirgy, M. J. (2012). Moderators of the self-congruity effect on consumer decision-making: A meta-analysis. *Journal of Business Research, 65*(8), 1179–1188.

Akiyama, H. (2010). Chōjujidai no kagaku to shakai no kōsō [The conception of science and society in the age of longevity]. *Kagaku (Science), 80*(1), 59–64.

Amos, C., Holmes, G., & Strutton, D. (2008). Exploring the relationship between celebrity endorser effects and advertising effectiveness. *International Journal of Advertising, 27*(2), 209–234.

Antony, S. P., Purwar, P. C., Kinra, N., & Moorthy, J. (2011). India: Opportunities and challenges of demographic transition. In F. Kohlbacher & C. Herstatt (eds), *The silver market phenomenon: Marketing and innovation in the aging society* (2nd ed., pp. 339–351). Heidelberg: Springer.

Arima, A. N. (2003). Gender stereotypes in Japanese television advertisements. *Sex Roles, 49*(1/2), 81–90.

Atkins, T. V., Jenkins, M. C., & Perkins, M. H. (1990/1991). Portrayal of persons in television commercials age 50 and older. *Psychology, A Journal of Human Behavior, 27/28*(4/1), 30–37.

Bai, X. (2014). Images of ageing in society: A literature review. *Population Ageing, 7*(3), 231–253.

Bandura, A. (2009). Social cognitive theory of mass communication. In J. Bryant & M. B. Oliver (eds), *Media effects: Advances in theory and research* (3rd ed., pp. 94–124). New York: Routledge.

Barak, B. (2009). Age identity: A cross-cultural global approach. *International Journal of Behavioral Development, 33*(1), 2–11.

Barnhart, M., & Peñaloza, L. (2013). Who are you calling old? Negotiating old age identity in the elderly consumption ensemble. *Journal of Consumer Research, 39*(6), 1133–1153.

Bartos, R. (1980). Over 49: The invisible consumer market. *Harvard Business Review, 58*(1), 140–148.

Bazzini, D. G., McIntosh, W. D., Smith, S. M., Cook, S., & Harris, C. (1997). The aging woman in popular film: Underrepresented, unattractive, unfriendly, and unintelligent. *Sex Roles, 36*(7/8), 531–543.

Beard, F. K. (2013). A history of comparative advertising in the United States. *Journalism & Communication Monographs, 15*(3), 114–216.

Bearden, W. O., Netemeyer, R. G., & Teel, J. E. (1989). Measurement of consumer susceptibility to interpersonal influence. *Journal of Consumer Research, 15*(4), 473–481.

Belk, R. W., & Bryce, W. J. (1986). Materialism and individual determinism in U.S. and Japanese print and television advertising. *Advances in Consumer Research, 13*(1), 568–572.

Bernhardt, K. L., & Kinnear, T. C. (1976). Profiling the senior citizen market. In B. B. Anderson (ed.), *Advances in Consumer Research* (Vol. 3, pp. 449–452). Cincinnati: Association for Consumer Research.

Berthon, P., Ewing, M., Pitt, L., & Berthon, J. P. (2003). Reframing replicative research in advertising. *International Journal of Advertising, 22*(4), 511–530.

Bradley, D. E., & Longino, C. F., Jr. (2001). How older people think about images of aging in advertising and the media. *Generations, 25*(3), 17–21.

Bristol, T. (1996). Persuading senior adults: The influence of endorser age on brand attitudes. *Journal of Current Issues & Research in Advertising, 18*(2), 59–67.

Burnett, J. J. (1989). Retirement versus age: Assessing the efficacy of retirement as a segmentation variable. *Journal of the Academy of Marketing Science, 17*(4), 333–343.

Burnett, J. J. (1991). Examining the media habits of the affluent elderly. *Journal of Advertising Research, 31*(5), 33–41.

Bush, A. J., Smith, R., & Martin, C. (1999). The influence of consumer socialization variables on attitude toward advertising: A comparison of African-Americans and Caucasians. *Journal of Advertising, 28*(3), 13–24.

Cacioppo, J. T., & Petty, R. E. (1985). Central and peripheral routes to persuasion: The role of message repetition. In L. F. Alwitt & A. A. Mitchell (eds), *Psychological processes and advertising effects: Theory, research and applications* (pp. 90–111). Hillsdale: Lawrence Erlbaum.

Carrigan, M., & Szmigin, I. (1999). In pursuit of youth: What's wrong with the older market? *Marketing Intelligence & Planning, 17*(5), 222–230.

Carrigan, M., & Szmigin, I. (2000a). Advertising in an ageing society. *Ageing & Society, 20*(2), 217–233.

Carrigan, M., & Szmigin, I. (2000b). The ethical advertising covenant: Regulating ageism in UK advertising. *International Journal of Advertising, 19*(4), 509–528.

Chand, M., & Tung, R. L. (2014). The aging of the world's population and its effects on global business. *Academy of Management Perspectives, 28*(4), 409–429.

Chang, C. (2008). Chronological age versus cognitive age for younger consumers. *Journal of Advertising, 37*(3), 19–32.

Cheng, H., & Kim, K. K. (2010). Research on advertising in Asia: A critical analysis of the articles published in major advertising and communication journals, 1990–2009. *Asian Journal of Communication, 20*(2), 248–263.

Choi, H., Paek, H.-J., & King, K. W. (2012). Are nutrient-content claims always effective? Match-up effects between product type and claim type in food advertising. *International Journal of Advertising, 31*(2), 421–443.

Choi, S. M., Lee, W.-N., & Kim, H.-J. (2005). Lessons from the rich and famous: A cross-cultural comparison of celebrity endorsement in advertising. *Journal of Advertising, 34*(2), 85–98.

Clark, R. L., Ogawa, N., Kondo, M., & Matsukura, R. (2010). Population decline, labor force stability, and the future of the Japanese economy. *European Journal of Population, 26*(2), 207–227.

Coffey, A. J. (2013). Understanding the invisibility of the Asian-American television audience: Why marketers often overlook an audience of "model" consumers. *Journal of Advertising Research, 53*(1), 101–118.

Coulmas, F. (2007). *Population decline and ageing in Japan – The social consequences*. London: Routledge.

Coulmas, F., Conrad, H., & Schad-Seifert, A. (2008). *The demographic challenge: A handbook about Japan*. Leiden: Brill.

Couper, M. P., & Miller, P. V. (2008). Web survey methods: Introduction. *Public Opinion Quarterly, 72*(5), 831–835.

Creighton, M. R. (1994). Images of foreigners in Japanese advertising. In J. Kovalio (ed.), *Japan in Focus* (pp. 225–240). Toronto: Captus University Publications.

Creighton, M. R. (1995). Imaging the other in Japanese advertising campaigns. In J. G. Carrier (ed.), *Occidentalism: Images of the West* (pp. 135–160). Oxford: Oxford University Press.

Creyer, E. H., & Ross, W. T., Jr. (1997). The influence of firm behavior on purchase intention: Do consumers really care about business ethics? *Journal of Consumer Marketing, 14*(6), 421–432.

Cuddy, A. J. C., Norton, M. I., & Fiske, S. T. (2005). This old stereotype: The pervasiveness and persistence of the elderly stereotype. *Journal of Social Issues, 61*(2), 267–285.

Cui, G., Chang, T.-S., & Joy, A. (2008). Consumers' attitudes toward marketing: A cross-cultural study of China and Canada. *Journal of International Consumer Marketing, 20*(3), 81–93.

Cui, G., Liu, H., Yang, X., & Wang, H. (2013). Culture, cognitive style and consumer response to informational vs. transformational advertising among East Asians: Evidence from the PRC. *Asia Pacific Business Review, 19*(1), 16–31.

Dallmann, K. M. (1998). *Kultur und Werbung: Eine theoretische und empirische Analyse zum Einfluß kultureller Dimensionen auf die Konzeption und Gestaltung von Werbung am Beispiel deutscher und japanischer Zeitschriftenwerbung. [Culture and advertising: A theoretical and empirical analysis of the impact of cultural dimensions on the conception and production of advertising in the case of German and Japanese magazine advertisements]*. Delmenhorst: Rieck.

Davies, R. J., & Ikeno, O. (2002). *The Japanese mind: Understanding contemporary Japanese culture*. Boston: Tuttle.

Davis, B., & French, W. A. (1989). Exploring advertising usage segments among the aged. *Journal of Advertising Research, 29*(1), 22–29.

Davis, R. H. (1971). Television and the older adult. *Journal of Broadcasting & Electronic Media, 15*(2), 153–160.

Davis, R. H. (1980). *Television and the aging audience*. University Park: Ethel Percy Andrus Gerontology Center.

Davis, R. H., & Westbrook, G. J. (1985). Television in the lives of the elderly: Attitudes and opinions. *Journal of Broadcasting & Electronic Media, 29*(2), 209–214.

Davison, W. (1983). The third-person effect in communication. *Public Opinion Quarterly, 47*(1), 1–15.

Day, E., & Stafford, M. R. (1997). Age-related cues in retail services advertising: Their effects on younger consumers. *Journal of Retailing, 73*(2), 211–233.

Dentsu. (2015). Advertising expenditure in Japan 2014. http://www.dentsu.com/books/pdf/expenditures_2014.pdf

Dentsu Senior Project. (2007). *Dankai Maketingu [Baby boomer marketing]*. Tokyo: Author.

DiBenedetto, A. C., Tamate, M., & Chandran, R. (1992). Developing creative advertising strategy for the Japanese marketplace. *Journal of Advertising Research, 32*(1), 39–48.

Donlon, M. M., Ashman, O., & Levy, B. R. (2005). Re-vision of older television characters: A stereotype-awareness intervention. *Journal of Social Issues, 61*(2), 307–319.

Drucker, P. F. (1951). Population trends and management policy. *Harvard Business Review, 29*(3), 73–79.

Drucker, P. F. (2002). *Managing in the next society*. New York: St. Martin's Press.

Dychtwald, K., & Flower, J. (1990). *The age wave: How the most important trend of our time can change your future*. Los Angeles: Bantam.

Easley, R. W., Madden, C. S., & Dunn, M. G. (2000). Conducting marketing science: The role of replication in the research process. *Journal of Business Research, 48*(1), 83–92.

Economist Intelligence Unit. (2011). A silver opportunity? Rising longevity and its implications for business. http://www.economistinsights.com/sites/default/files/legacy/mgthink/downloads/EIU-Axa_Longevity_Web.pdf

Enda, K., Shibata, H., Watanabe, S., & Sugisawa, H. (2007). Hōsōjin no kōreisha ni kansuru ishiki [Awareness of older people among people working in broadcasting]. *Ōyōrōnengaku (Applied Gerontology), 1*(1), 54–67.

Erdogan, B. Z. (1999). Celebrity endorsement: A literature review. *Journal of Marketing Management, 15*(4), 291–314.

Featherstone, M., & Wernick, A. (eds). (1995). *Images of aging: Cultural representations of later life*. London: Routledge.

Ferle, C. L., & Lee, W.-N. (2003). Attitudes toward advertising. *Journal of International Consumer Marketing, 15*(2), 5–23.

Festervand, T. A., & Lumpkin, J. R. (1985). Response of elderly consumers to their portrayal by advertisers. *Current Issues & Research in Advertising, 8*(2), 203–226.

Festinger, L. (1954). A theory of social comparison processes. *Human Relations, 7*(2), 117–140.

Fields, G. (1983). *From bonsai to Levi's: When West meets East: An insider's surprising account of how the Japanese live.* New York: Mentor.

Formanek, S. (2008). Traditional concepts and images of old age in Japan. In F. Coulmas, H. Conrad, A. Schad-Seifert & G. Vogt (eds), *The demographic challenge: A handbook about Japan* (pp. 323–343). Leiden: Brill.

Frith, K. T., & Mueller, B. (2010). *Advertising and societies: Global issues* (2nd ed.). New York: Peter Lang.

Frith, K. T., Shaw, P., & Cheng, H. (2005). The construction of beauty: A cross-cultural analysis of women's magazine advertising. *Journal of Communication, 55*(1), 56–70.

Fukawa, H. (2008). Poverty among the elderly. In F. Coulmas, H. Conrad, A. Schad-Seifert & G. Vogt (eds), *The demographic challenge: A handbook about Japan* (pp. 921–931). Leiden: Brill.

Fullerton, J. A., & Kendrick, A. (2000). Portrayal of men and women in U.S. Spanish-language television commercials. *Journalism & Mass Communication Quarterly, 77*(1), 128–142.

Fung, H. H. (2013). Aging in culture. *The Gerontologist, 53*(3), 369–377.

Furnham, A., & Bitar, N. (1993). The stereotyped portrayal of men and women in British television advertisements. *Sex Roles, 29*(3/4), 297–310.

Furnham, A., & Farragher, E. (2000). A cross-cultural content analysis of sex-role stereotyping in television advertisements: A comparison between Great Britain and New Zealand. *Journal of Broadcasting & Electronic Media, 44*(3), 415–436.

Furnham, A., & Mak, T. (1999). Sex-role stereotyping in television commercials: A review and comparison of fourteen studies done on five continents over 25 years. *Sex Roles, 41*(5/6), 413–437.

Furnham, A., Mak, T., & Tanidjojo, L. (2000). An Asian perspective on the portrayal of men and women in television advertisements: Studies from Hong Kong and Indonesian television. *Journal of Applied Social Psychology, 30*(11), 2341–2364.

Ganahl, D. J., Prinsen, T. J., & Netzley, S. B. (2003). A content analysis of prime time commercials: A contextual framework of gender representation. *Sex Roles, 49*(9/10), 545–551.

Garcia, E., & Yang, K. C. C. (2006). Consumer response to sexual appeals in cross-cultural advertisements. *Journal of International Consumer Marketing, 19*(2), 29–52.

Garstka, T. A., & Schmitt, M. T. (2004). How young and older adults differ in their responses to perceived age discrimination. *Psychology and Aging, 19*(2), 236–335.

Gerbner, G. (1993). Learning productive aging as a social role: The lessons of television. In S. A. Bass, F. G. Caro & Y. Che (eds), *Achieving a productive aging society* (pp. 207–220). Westport: Auburn House.

Gerbner, G. (1998). Cultivation analysis: An overview. *Mass Communication & Society, 1*(3), 175–194.

Gerbner, G., Gross, L., Morgan, M., & Signorielli, N. (1981). Aging with television commercials: Images on television commercials and dramatic programming, 1977–1979. Philadelphia: The Annenberg School of Communications, University of Pennsylvania.

Gerbner, G., Gross, L., Signorielli, N., & Morgan, M. (1980). Aging with television: Images on television drama and conceptions of social reality. *Journal of Communication, 30*(1), 37–47.

Giles, H., Bourghis, R. Y., & Taylor, D. M. (1977). Towards a theory of language in ethnic group relations. In H. Giles (ed.), *Language, ethnicity and intergroup relations* (pp. 307–348). London: Academic Press.

Gilly, M. C. (1988). Sex roles in advertising: A comparision of television advertisements in Australia, Mexico, and the United States. *Journal of Marketing, 52*(2), 75–85.

Goldstein, S. (1968). The aged segment of the market, 1950 and 1960. *Journal of Marketing, 32*(2), 62–68.

Görtzen, U. (1995). *Die Entwicklung der japanischen Werbewirtschaft in der Nachkriegszeit (1950–1990): Von der „reinen Produktwerbung" zum „kreativen Unsinn" [The development of the Japanese advertising industry in the postwar era (1950–1990): From pure product advertising to "creative nonsense"].* Marburg: Japan-Zentrum der Philipps-Universität Marburg.

Greco, A. J. (1988). The elderly as communicators: Perceptions of advertising practitioners. *Journal of Advertising Research, 28*(3), 39–46.

Greco, A. J. (1989). Representation of the elderly in advertising: Crisis or inconsequence? *The Journal of Consumer Marketing, 6*(1), 37–44.

Greco, A. J. (1993). The incidence and portrayal of the elderly in television advertising. *The Journal of Marketing – Theory and Practice, 2*(1), 140–154.

Greco, A. J., & Johnson, E. B. (1997). Supermarket shoppers' response to mature models in point-of-purchase displays. *Journal of Food Products Marketing, 4*(3), 9–23.

Greco, A. J., & Swayne, L. E. (1992). Sales response of elderly consumers to point-of-purchase advertising. *Journal of Advertising Research, 32*(5), 43–53.

Greco, A. J., Swayne, L. E., & Johnson, E. B. (1997). Will older models turn off shoppers? *International Journal of Advertising, 16*(1), 27–36.

Guido, G., Peluso, A. M., & Moffa, V. (2011). Beardedness in advertising: Effects on endorsers' credibility and purchase intention. *Journal of Marketing Communications, 17*(1), 37–49.

Gunter, B. (1998). *Understanding the older consumer: The grey market.* London: Routledge.

Gwinner, K. P., & Stephens, N. (2001). Testing the implied mediational role of cognitive age. *Psychology & Marketing, 18*(10), 1031–1048.

Haarmann, H. (1984). The role of ethnocultural stereotypes and foreign languages in Japanese commercials. *International Journal of the Sociology of Language, 50*, 101–121.

Haboush, A., Warren, C. S., & Benuto, L. (2012). Beauty, ethnicity, and age: Does internalization of mainstrem media ideals influence attitudes towards older adults? *Sex Roles, 66*(9/10), 668–676.

Haehling von Lanzenauer, N. (1999). *Werbung in Japan: Eine Untersuchung der Werbewirtschaft und Werbegestaltung unter besonderer Berücksichtigung von Unternehmenswerbung [Advertising in Japan: An analysis of the advertising industry and advertising design with special emphasis on institutional advertising]*. Doctoral thesis, Free University, Berlin.

Hagiwara, S. (2004). Nihon no terebi kōkoku ni arawareru gaikoku imēji no dōkō [Trends of foreign images in Japanese television commercials]. *Keio Media and Communications Research, 54*, 5–26.

Hagiwara, S., Kohlbacher, F., Prieler, M., & Arima, A. (2010). Nihon no terebi ni okeru kōreisha hyōshō to kōreisha shijō he no apurōchi: Terebi CM no naiyo bunseki to kōkoku kankeisha oyobi shōhisha no ishiki chōsa [The representation of elderly people and the approaches to the silver market in Japanese television commercials: A content analysis on TV commercials, and a survey among advertising agencies and consumers]. Tokyo: Yoshida Hideo Memorial Foundation.

Hagiwara, S., Prieler, M., Kohlbacher, F., & Arima, A. (2009). Nihon no terebi CM ni okeru kōreishazō no hensen: 1997nen to 2007nen no hikaku [Changes in the representation of older adults in Japanese TV commercials: Comparing the years 1997 and 2007]. *Keio Media and Communications Research, 59*, 113–129.

Hajjar, W. J. (1997). The image of aging in television commercials: An update for the 1990s. In H. S. Noor Al-Deen (ed.), *Cross-cultural communication and aging in the United States* (pp. 231–244). Mahwah: Lawrence Erlbaum.

Hakuhodo. (2003). *Kyodai shijō "erudā" no tanjō [The birth of the colossal "elder market"]*. Tokyo: Purejidentosha.

Hakuhodo Elder Business Suishinshitsu. (2006). *Dankai sādo wēbu: Atarashii otona bunka ga umareru [The third babyboomer wave: The birth of a new adult culture]*. Tokyo: Kobundo.

Hall, E. T. (1976). *Beyond culture*. New York: Anchor Books.

Harper, S. (2014). Economic and social implications of aging societies. *Science, 346*, 587–591.

Harrington, C. L., Bielby, D. D., & Bardo, A. R. (eds). (2014). *Aging, media, and culture*. Lanham: Lexington.

Harwood, J. (2007). *Understanding communication and aging: Developing knowledge and awareness*. Thousand Oaks: Sage.

Harwood, J., & Anderson, K. (2002). The presence and portrayal of social groups on prime-time television. *Communication Reports, 15*(2), 81–97.

Harwood, J., Giles, H., Ota, H., Pierson, H. D., Gallois, C., Ng, S. H., et al. (1996). College students' trait ratings of three age groups around the Pacific Rim. *Journal of Cross-Cultural Gerontology, 11*(4), 307–317.

Hayes, A. F. (2005). *Statistical methods for communication science*. Mahwah: Lawrence Erlbaum.

Healey, T., & Ross, K. (2002). Growing old invisibly: Older viewers talk television. *Media, Culture & Society, 24*(1), 105–120.

Hesse, B. W., Nelson, D. E., Kreps, G. L., Croyle, R. T., Arora, N. K., Rimer, B. K., et al. (2005). Trust and sources of health information: The impact of the Internet and its implications for health care providers: Findings from the first health information national trends. *Archives of Internal Medicine, 165*(22), 2618–2624.

Hiemstra, R., Goodman, M., Middlemiss, M. A., Vosko, R., & Ziegler, N. (1983). How older people are portrayed in television advertising: Implications for educators. *Educational Gerontology, 9*(2/3), 111–122.

Higgs, B., & Milner, L. (2006). *Portrayals of maturity in Australian television commercials: A benchmark study*. Paper presented at the 6th Annual Hawaii International Business Conference, Hawaii.

Hilt, M. L., & Lipschultz, J. H. (2004). Elderly Americans and the Internet: E-mail, TV news, information and entertainment websites. *Educational Gerontology, 30*(1), 57–72.

Hiyoshi, A. (2001). Terebi kōkoku no naka no gaikokujin tōjō jinbutsuzō to sono henka [Changes in the image of "foreign" characters in television advertising]. *Nenpō Shakaigakuronshū (Kantō Shakaigakkai), 14*(June), 89–101.

Hoffmann, S., Liebermann, S. C., & Schwarz, U. (2012). Ads for mature consumers: The importance of addressing the changing self-view between the age groups 50+ and 60+. *Journal of Promotion Management, 18*(1), 60–82.

Hofstede, G. (2001). *Culture's consequences: Comparing values, behaviors, institutions, and organizations across nations* (2nd ed.). London: Sage.

Holden, T. J. M. (2002). Semiotic literacy, post-modernity, Malaysia and Japan: How television advertising reveals political-economic development and change. *Interdisciplinary Information Sciences, 8*(1), 1–14.

Hommerich, C. (2012). The advent of vulnerability: Japan's free fall through its porous safety net. *Japan Forum, 24*(2), 205–232.

Hong, J. W., Muderrisoglu, A., & Zinkhan, G. M. (1987). Cultural differences and advertising expression: A comparative content analysis of Japanese and U.S. magazine advertising. *Journal of Advertising, 16*(1), 55–68.

Hong, J. W., & Zinkhan, G. M. (1995). Self-concept and advertising effectiveness: The influence of congruency, conspicuousness, and response mode. *Psychology & Marketing, 12*(1), 53–77.

Horiuchi, Y., Shibata, H., Watanabe, S., & Haga, H. (2010). Kigyō ni okeru kōreishakanren no shakaikōkenkatsudō: Genjō and kongo no kadai [Corporate CSR activities related to older people: Status quo and future tasks]. *Ōyōrōnengaku (Applied Gerontology), 4*(1), 82–90.

Horton, D., & Wohl, R. R. (1956). Mass communication and para-social interaction: Observations on intimacy at a distance. *Psychiatry, 19*(3), 215–229.

Hoskins, C., McFayden, S., & Finn, A. (2004). *Media economics: Applying economics to new and traditional media*. Thousand Oaks: Sage.

Huang, C.-S. (2013). Undergraduate students' knowledge about aging and attitutudes toward older adults in East and West: A socio-economic and cultural exploration. *International Journal of Aging and Human Development, 77*(1), 59–76.

Hubbard, R., & Armstrong, J. S. (1994). Replications and extensions in marketing: Rarely published but quite contrary. *International Journal of Research in Marketing, 11*(3), 233–248.

Huber, F., Meyer, F., Vogel, J., Weihrauch, A., & Hamprecht, J. (2013). Endorser age and stereotypes: Consequences on brand age. *Journal of Business Research, 66*(2), 207–215.

Hummert, M. L. (1990). Multiple stereotypes of elderly and young adults: A comparison of structure and evaluations. *Psychology and Aging, 5*(2), 182–193.

Hunter, J. E. (2001). The desperate need for replications. *Journal of Consumer Research, 28*(1), 149–158.

Ilieva, J., Baron, S., & Healey, N. M. (2002). Online surveys in marketing research: Pros and cons. *International Journal of Market Research, 44*(3), 361–376.

Innes, J. M., & Zeitz, H. (1988). The public's view of the impact of the mass media: A test of the "third-person" effect. *European Journal of Social Psychology, 18*(5), 457–463.

Iwao, S. (1984). Gaikokujin moderu kiyō appoint jittai [The truth of appointing foreign models]. *Keiō Gijuku Daigaku Shimbun Kenkyūjo Nenpō, 23*, 81–92.

Johansson, J. K. (1994). The sense of "nonsense": Japanese TV advertising. *Journal of Advertising, 23*(1), 17–26.

Kamins, M. A. (1990). An investigation into the "match-up" hypothesis in celebrity advertising: When beauty may be only skin deep. *Journal of Advertising, 19*(1), 4–13.

Kamins, M. A., & Gupta, K. (1994). Congruence between spokesperson and product type: A matchup hypothesis perspective. *Psychology & Marketing, 11*(6), 569–586.

Kawashima, N. (2006). Advertising agencies, media and consumer market: The changing quality of TV advertising in Japan. *Media, Culture & Society, 28*(3), 393–410.

Keown, C. F., Jacobs, L. W., Schmidt, R. W., & Ghymn, K.-I. (1992). Information content of advertising in the United States, Japan, South Korea, and the People's Republic of China. *International Journal of Advertising, 11*(3), 257–267.

Kessler, E.-M., Rakoczy, K., & Staudinger, U. M. (2004). The portrayal of older people in prime time television series: The match with gerontological evidence. *Ageing & Society, 24*(4), 531–552.

Kessler, E.-M., Schwender, C., & Bowen, C. E. (2010). The portrayal of older people's social participation on German prime-time TV advertisements. *Journal of Gerontology: Social Sciences, 65B*(1), 97–106.

Kingston, J. (2013). *Contemporary Japan: History, politics, and social change since the 1980s* (2nd ed.). Chichester: Wiley-Blackwell.

Kite, M. E., & Johnson, B. T. (1988). Attitudes toward older and younger adults: A meta-analysis. *Psychology and Aging, 3*(3), 233–244.

Klippel, R. E., & Sweeney, T. W. (1974). The use of information sources by the aged consumer. *The Gerontologist, 14*(2), 163–166.

Klock, S. J., & Traylor, M. B. (1983). Older & younger models in advertising to older consumers: An advertising effectiveness experiment. *Akron Business and Economic Review, 14*(1), 48–52.

Kohlbacher, F. (2011). Business implications of demographic change in Japan: Chances and challenges for human resource and marketing management. In F. Coulmas & R. Lützeler (eds), *Imploding populations in Japan and Germany: A comparison* (pp. 269–294). Leiden: Brill.

Kohlbacher, F. (2013). The business of aging. *Huffington Post*, 02/28/2013. http://www.huffingtonpost.com/florian-kohlbacher-phd/the-business-of-aging_b_2784549.html

Kohlbacher, F., & Chéron, E. J. (2012). Understanding "silver" consumers through cognitive age, health condition, financial status, and personal values: Empirical evidence from the world's most mature market Japan. *Journal of Consumer Behaviour, 11*(3), 179–188.

Kohlbacher, F., Gudorf, P., & Herstatt, C. (2011). Japan's growing silver market – An attractive business opportunity for foreign companies? In M. Boppel, S. Boehm & S. Kunisch (eds), *From grey to silver: Managing the demographic change successfully* (pp. 189–205). Heidelberg: Springer.

Kohlbacher, F., & Hang, C. (2011). Applying the disruptive innovation framework to the silver market: Technology adoption and deployment for older consumers. *Ageing International, 36*(1), 82–101.

Kohlbacher, F., & Herstatt, C. (2008). Preface and Introduction. In F. Kohlbacher & C. Herstatt (eds), *The silver market phenomenon: Business opportunities in an era of demographic change* (pp. xi–xxv). Heidelberg: Springer.

Kohlbacher, F., & Herstatt, C. (eds). (2011). *The silver market phenomenon: Marketing and innovation in the aging society* (2nd ed.). Heidelberg: Springer.

Kohlbacher, F., Herstatt, C., & Levsen, N. (2015). Golden opportunities for silver innovation: How demographic changes give rise to entrepreneurial opportunities to meet the needs of older people. *Technovation, 39/40*, 73–82.

Kohlbacher, F., Herstatt, C., & Schweisfurth, T. (2011). Product development for the silver market. In F. Kohlbacher & C. Herstatt (eds), *The silver market phenomenon: Marketing and innovation in the aging society* (2nd ed., pp. 3–13). Heidelberg: Springer.

Kohlbacher, F., & Hideg, A. (2011). The easy-easy way – The Raku-Raku Phone: Simple communication that is simply successful. *Marketing Management, 20*(1), 38–43.

Kohlbacher, F., & Matsuno, K. (2012). Firms' (non-)responses to obvious but less-controllable external forces. Paper presented at the 24th Annual Conference of the Society for the Advancement of Socio-Economics (SASE), Cambridge, MA.

Kohlbacher, F., & Mollenhauer, H. (2013). Balancing supply and demand in the job market for older workers. *Japan Close-Up, August*, 19–20.

Kohlbacher, F., Prieler, M., & Hagiwara, S. (2011a). *Consumer response to the portrayal of older people in TV advertising: Empirical evidence from Japan.* Paper presented at the Asia Pacific Advances in Consumer Research (AP-ACR) Conference 2011, Bejing, PR China.

Kohlbacher, F., Prieler, M., & Hagiwara, S. (2011b). The use of older models in Japanese advertising: Practitioner perspective vs. consumer opinions. *Keio Communication Review, 33*, 25–42.

Kohlbacher, F., Prieler, M., & Hagiwara, S. (2014). Japan's demographic revolution? A study of advertising practitioners' views on stereotypes. *Asia Pacific Business Review, 20*(2), 249–268.

Kohlbacher, F., & Rabe, B. (2015). Leading the way into the future: The development of a (lead) market for care robotics in Japan. *International Journal of Technology, Policy and Management, 15*(1), 21–44.

Kohlbacher, F., & Weihrauch, A. (2009). Japan's silver market phenomenon: Golden opportunity or rusty reality? *Japan Close-Up, May 2009*, 18–23.

Kolbe, R. H., & Burnett, M. S. (1992). Perceptions of elderly and young adult respondents toward the portrayal of the elderly in advertising: Implications to advertising managers. *The Journal of Marketing Management, 2*(1), 76–85.

Korzenny, F., & Neuendorf, K. (1980). Television viewing and self-concept of the elderly. *Journal of Communication, 30*(1), 71–80.

Koyano, W. (1989). Japanese attitudes toward the elderly: A review of research findings. *Journal of Cross-Cultural Gerontology, 4*(4), 335–345.

Koyano, W. (1997). Myths and facts of aging in Japan. In S. Formanek & S. Linhart (eds), *Aging: Asian concepts and experiences – Past and present* (pp. 213–227). Vienna: Verlag der österreichischen Akademie der Wissenschaften.

Kozakai, T. (1996). *Ibunka juyō no paradokkusu [The paradox of foreign culture acceptance]*. Tokyo: Asahi Shimbunsha.

Kulik, C. T., Ryan, S., Harper, S., & George, G. (2014). Aging populations and management. *Academy of Management Journal, 57*(4), 929–935.

Lambert-Pandraud, R., & Laurent, G. (2010). Why do older consumers buy older brands? The role of attachment and declining innovativeness. *Journal of Marketing, 74*(5), 104–121.

Lambert-Pandraud, R., Laurent, G., & Lapersonne, E. (2005). Repeat purchasing of new automobiles by older consumers: Empirical evidence and interpretations. *Journal of Marketing, 69*(2), 97–113.

Langmeyer, L. (1984). Senior citizens and television advertisements: A research note. *Current Issues & Research in Advertising, 7*(1), 167–178.

Langmeyer, L. (1993). Advertising images of mature adults: An update. *Journal of Current Issues & Research in Advertising, 15*(2), 81–91.

Laroche, M., Cleveland, M., & Browne, E. (2004). Exploring age-related differences in information acquisition for a gift purchase. *Journal of Economic Psychology, 25*(1), 61–95.

Lee, B.-K., Kim, B.-C., & Han, S. (2006). The portrayal of older people in television advertisements: A cross-cultural content analysis of the United States and Korea. *International Journal of Aging and Human Development, 63*(4), 279–297.

Lee, M. M., Carpenter, B., & Meyers, L. S. (2007). Representations of older adults in television advertisements. *Journal of Aging Studies, 21*(1), 23–30.

Lee, W.-N., Choi, S. M., & Tsai, W. S. (2007). *Celebrity advertising in Japan and Korea: Doing it the Asian way?* Paper presented at the 2007 Asia-Pacific Conference of the American Academy of Advertising.

Levy, B. R. (1996). Improving memory in old age through implicit self-stereotyping. *Journal of Personality and Social Psychology, 71*(6), 1092–1107.

Levy, B. R. (1999). The inner self of the Japanese elderly: A defense against negative stereotypes of aging. *International Journal of Aging and Human Development, 48*(2), 131–144.

Levy, B. R. (2003). Mind matters: Cognitive and physical effects of aging self-stereotypes. *Journal of Gerontology: Psychological Sciences, 58B*(4), 203–211.

Levy, B. R., Hausdorff, J. M., Hencke, R., & Wei, J. Y. (2000). Reducing cardiovascular stress with positive self-stereotypes of aging. *Journal of Gerontology, 55B*(4), 205–213.

Levy, B. R., Slade, M. D., & Gill, T. M. (2006). Hearing decline predicted by elders' stereotypes. *Journal of Gerontology, 61B*(2), 82–87.

Levy, B. R., Slade, M. D., & Kasl, S. V. (2002). Longitudinal benefit of positive self-perceptions of aging on functional health. *Journal of Gerontology, 57B*(5), 409–417.

Levy, B. R., Slade, M. D., Kunkel, S. R., & Kasl, S. V. (2002). Longevity increased by positive self-perceptions of aging. *Journal of Personality and Social Psychology, 83*(2), 261–270.

Lin, C. A. (1993). Cultural differences in message strategies: A comparison between American and Japanese TV commercials. *Journal of Advertising Research, 33*(4), 40–48.

Lin, C. A., & Salwen, M. B. (1995). Product information strategies of American and Japanese television advertisements. *International Journal of Advertising, 14*(1), 55–64.

Lumpkin, J. R., & Festervand, T. A. (1988). Purchase information sources of the elderly. *Journal of Advertising Research, 27*(6), 31–44.

Lundstrom, W. J., & Sciglimpaglia, D. (1977). Sex role portrayals in advertising. *Journal of Marketing, 41*(3), 72–79.

Luyt, R. (2011). Representation of gender in South African television advertising: A content analysis. *Sex Roles, 65*(5/6), 356–370.

Lynch, J., & Schuler, D. (1994). The matchup effect of spokesperson and product congruency: A schema theory interpretation. *Psychology & Marketing, 11*(5), 417–445.

Madden, C. S., Caballero, M. J., & Matsukubo, S. (1986). Analysis of information content in U.S. and Japanese magazine advertising. *Journal of Advertising, 15*(3), 38–45.

Madden, C. S., Easley, R. W., & Dunn, M. G. (1995). How journal editors view replication research. *Journal of Advertising, 24*(4), 77–87.

Magnus, G. (2009). *The age of aging: How demographics are changing the global economy and our world*. Singapore: John Wiley & Sons.

Mares, M.-L., & Cantor, J. (1992). Elderly viewers' responses to televised portrayals of old age: Empathy and mood management versus social comparison. *Communication Research, 19*(4), 459–478.

Martin, D. (2005). Advertiser acculturation in Japan: Examples from foreign actors. *Asia Pacific Journal of Marketing and Logistics, 17*(2), 71–83.

Martin, D., & Woodside, A. G. (2007). Dochakuka: Melding global inside local: Foreign-domestic advertising assimilation in Japan. *Journal of Global Marketing, 21*(1), 19–32.

Mason, J. B., & Bearden, W. O. (1978). Profiling the shopping behavior of elderly consumers. *The Gerontologist, 18*(5), 454–461.

Mastro, D. E., & Stern, S. R. (2003). Representations of race in television commercials: A content analysis of prime-time advertising. *Journal of Broadcasting & Electronic Media, 47*(4), 638–647.

Mathur, A. (1999). Adoption of technological innovations by the elderly: A consumer socialization perspective. *Journal of Marketing Management, 9*(3), 21–35.

Mathur, A., & Moschis, G. P. (2005). Antecedents of cognitive age: A replication and extension. *Psychology & Marketing, 22*(12), 969–994.

Mazis, M. B., Ringold, D. J., Perry, E. S., & Denman, D. W. (1992). Perceived age and attractiveness of models in cigarette advertisements. *Journal of Marketing, 56*(1), 22–37.

McCaughan, D. (2015). Aging Asia: Myths about mature markets. *Research World, 52*(May/June), 22–25.

McCracken, G. (1989). Who is the celebrity endorser? Cultural foundations of the endorsement process. *Journal of Consumer Research, 16*(3), 310–321.

McCreery, J. (2000). *Japanese consumer behavior: From worker bees to wary shoppers.* Honolulu: University of Hawai'i Press.

Miller, D. W., Leyell, T. S., & Mazachek, J. (2004). Stereotypes of the elderly in U.S. television commercials from the 1950s to the 1990s. *International Journal of Aging and Human Development, 58*(4), 315–340.

Miller, P. N., Miller, D. W., McKibbin, E. M., & Pettys, G. L. (1999). Stereotypes of the elderly in magazine advertisements 1956–1996. *International Journal of Aging and Human Development, 49*(4), 319–337.

Milliman, R. E., & Erffmeyer, R. C. (1990). Improving advertising aimed at seniors. *Journal of Advertising Research, 29*(6), 31–36.

Milner, L. M., & Collins, J. M. (2000). Sex-role portrayals and the gender of nations. *Journal of Advertising, 29*(1), 67–79.

Milner, L. M., & Higgs, B. (2004). Gender sex-role portrayals in international television advertising over time: The Australian experience. *Journal of Current Issues & Research in Advertising, 26*(2), 81–95.

Ministry of Internal Affairs and Communications. (1995). Census 1995. http://www.stat.go.jp/english/data/kokusei/1995/1513.htm

Ministry of Internal Affairs and Communications. (2005). Census 2005. http://www.e-stat.go.jp/SG1/estat/ListE.do?bid=000001005118&cycode=0

Ministry of Internal Affairs and Communications. (2009). 2008 survey on ICT usage trends. http://www.e-stat.go.jp/SG1/estat/ListE.do?lid=000001058621 and http://www.stat.go.jp/data/jinsui/tsuki/index.htm

Moeran, B. (1996). *A Japanese advertising agency: An anthropology of media and markets.* Honolulu: University of Hawai'i Press.

Mooney, S. (2000). *5,110 days in Tokyo and everything's hunky-dory: The marketer's guide to advertising in Japan.* Westport: Quorum.

Morgan, M., Shanahan, J., & Signorielli, N. (2009). Growing up with television: Cultivation processes. In J. Bryant & M. B. Oliver (eds), *Media effects: Advances in theory and research* (3rd ed., pp. 34–49). New York: Routledge.

Morimoto, M., & Chang, S. (2009). Western and Asian models in Japanese fashion magazine ads: The relationship with brand origins and international versus domestic magazines. *Journal of International Consumer Marketing, 21*(3), 173–187.

Moschis, G. P. (1987). *Consumer socialization: A life-cycle perspective.* Lexington: Lexington Books.

Moschis, G. P. (1994). *Marketing strategies for the mature market.* Westport: Quorum Books.

Moschis, G. P. (1996). *Gerontographics: Life-stage segmentation for marketing strategy development.* Westport: Quorum Books.

Moschis, G. P. (2003). Marketing to older adults: An updated overview of present knowledge and practice. *Journal of Consumer Marketing, 20*(6), 516–525.

Moschis, G. P. (2007). Life course perspectives on consumer behavior. *Journal of the Academy of Marketing Science, 35*(2), 295–307.

Moschis, G. P. (2012). Consumer behavior in later life: Current knowledge, issues, and new directions for research. *Psychology & Marketing, 29*(2), 57–75.

Moschis, G. P., Lee, E., & Mathur, A. (1997). Targeting the mature market: Opportunities and challenges. *Journal of Consumer Marketing, 14*(4), 282–293.

Moschis, G. P., & Mathur, A. (2006). Older consumer responses to marketing stimuli: The power of subjective age. *Journal of Advertising Research, 46*(3), 339–346.

Moschis, G. P., Mathur, A., & Smith, R. B. (1993). Older consumers' orientations toward age-based marketing stimuli. *Journal of the Academy of Marketing Science, 21*(3), 195–205.

Moschis, G. P., & Moore, R. L. (1982). A longitudinal study of television advertising effects. *Journal of Consumer Research, 9*(3), 279–286.

Mueller, B. (1987). Reflections of culture: An analysis of Japanese and American advertising appeals. *Journal of Advertising Research, 27*(3), 51–59.

Mueller, B. (1991). An analysis of information content in standardized vs. specialized multinational advertisements. *Journal of International Business Studies, 22*(1), 23–39.

Mueller, B. (1992). Standardization vs. specialization: An examination of Westernization in Japanese advertising. *Journal of Advertising Research, 32*(1), 15–24.

Muramatsu, N., & Akiyama, H. (2011). Japan: Super-aging society preparing for the future. *The Gerontologist, 51*(4), 425–432.

Murata, H. (2012). *Shinia shifuto no shōgeki [The senior shift shock].* Tokyo: Diamond.

Nakanishi, M. (2002). TV commercials as cultural performance: The case of Japan. In R. T. Donahue (ed.), *Exploring Japaneseness: On Japanese enactments of culture and consciousness.* Westport: Ablex.

Nam, K., Lee, G., & Hwang, J.-S. (2011). Gender stereotypes depicted by Western and Korean advertising models in Korean adolescent girls' magazines. *Sex Roles, 64*(3/4), 223–237.

Namba, K. (2002). Comparative studies in USA and Japanese advertising during the post-war era. *International Journal of Japanese Sociology, 11*(1), 56–71.

Nelson, S. L., & Smith, R. B. (1988). The influence of model age or older consumers' reactions to print advertising. *Current Issues & Research in Advertising, 11*(1), 189–212.

Neto, F., & Pinto, I. (1998). Gender stereotypes in Portuguese television advertisements. *Sex Roles, 39*(1/2), 153–164.

Neuendorf, K. A. (2011). Content analysis – A methodological primer for gender research. *Sex Roles, 64*(3/4), 276–289.

Nihon Shimbun Kyokai. (2010). *Bēsumedia to seikatsusha – Atarashii hyōkajiku wo kangaeru: 2009nen zenkoku media sesshoku hyōka chōsa hōkokusho [Thinking about a new evaluation axis of life styles based on media usage: 2009 nationwide media contact and evaluation survey report].* Tokyo: Author.

Nikkei Kokoku Kenkyujo. (2009). *Kōkoku hakusho [Advertising white paper].* Tokyo: Nihon Keizai Shimbun.

Nikkei Kokoku Kenkyujo. (2010). *Kōkoku hakusho [Advertising white paper].* Tokyo: Nihon Keizai Shimbun.

Nikkei Kokoku Kenkyujo. (2014). *Kōkoku hakusho [Advertising white paper].* Tokyo: Nihon Keizai Shimbun.

Nikkei Weekly. (2010). Boomers wield financial clout. *January 11, 2010*, p. 3.

Nishimasa. (2006). Terebi no kōkoku moderu ni kan suru [About advertising models in television]. http://plusd.itmedia.co.jp/lifestyle/articles/0601/27/news072.html

Nussbaum, J. F., Pecchioni, L. L., Robinson, J. D., & Thompson, T. L. (2000). *Communication and aging* (2nd ed.). Mahwah: Lawrence Erlbaum Associates.

Nyren, C. (2007). *Advertising to baby boomers.* Ithaca: Paramount Market Publishing.

O'Guinn, T. C., & Shrum, L. J. (1997). The role of television in the construction of consumer reality. *Journal of Consumer Research, 23*(4), 278–294.

O'Leary, J. S. (1993). A new look at Japan's honorable elders. *Journal of Aging Studies, 7*(1), 1–24.

Oakes, S., & North, A. C. (2011). The impact of narrator age congruity on responses to a radio advertisement. *Journal of Marketing Communications, 17*(3), 183–194.

Ohtake, F. (2008). The ageing society and economic inequality. In F. Coulmas, H. Conrad, A. Schad-Seifert & G. Vogt (eds), *The demographic challenge: A handbook about Japan* (pp. 899–919). Leiden: Brill.

Okazaki, S., & Mueller, B. (2008). Evolution in the usage of localised appeals in Japanese and American print advertising. *International Journal of Advertising, 27*(5), 771–798.

Okazaki, S., & Mueller, B. (2011). The impact of the lost decade on advertising in Japan: A grounded theory approach. *International Journal of Advertising, 30*(2), 205–232.

Okazaki, S., Mueller, B., & Taylor, C. R. (2010). Global consumer culture positioning: Testing perceptions of soft-sell and hard-sell advertising appeals between U.S. and Japanese consumers. *Journal of International Marketing, 18*(2), 20–34.

Ong, F. S., & Chang, H. K. (2009). Older people as models in advertisements: A cross-cultural content analysis of two Asian countries. *Journal of Business & Policy Research, 4*(2), 1–15.

Paek, H.-J., Nelson, M. R., & Vilela, A. M. (2011). Examination of gender-role portrayals in television advertising across seven countries. *Sex Roles, 64*(3/4), 192–207.

Painter, A. A. (1996). Japanese daytime television, popular culture, and ideology. In J. W. Treat (ed.), *Contemporary Japan and popular culture* (pp. 197–234). Richmond: Curzon.

Palmore, E. (1998). *Facts on Aging Quiz* (2nd ed.). New York: Springer.

Palmore, E., & Maeda, D. (1985). *The honorable elders revisited: A revised cross-cultural analysis of ageing in Japan.* Durham: Duke University Press.

Passuth, P. M., & Cook, F. L. (1985). Effects of television viewing on knowledge and attitudes about older adults: A critical reexamination. *The Gerontologist, 25*(1), 69–77.

Patterson, I. (2007). Information sources used by older adults for decision making about tourist and travel destinations. *International Journal of Consumer Studies, 31*(5), 528–533.

Perry, V. G., & Wolburg, J. M. (2011). Aging gracefully: Emerging issues for public policy and consumer welfare. *Journal of Consumer Affairs, 45*(3), 365–371.

Peterson, R. T., & Ross, D. T. (1997). A content analysis of the portrayal of mature individuals in television commercials. *Journal of Business Ethics, 16*(4), 425–433.

Petroshius, S. M., & Crocker, K. E. (1989). An empirical analysis of spokesperson characteristics on advertisement and product evaluations. *Journal of the Academy of Marketing Science, 17*(3), 217–225.

Pew Research Center. (2014). Attitudes about aging: A global perspective. http://www.pewglobal.org/2014/01/30/attitudes-about-aging-a-global-perspective/

Phillips, L. W., & Sternthal, B. (1977). Age differences in information processing: A perspective on the aged consumer. *Journal of Marketing Research, 14*(4), 444–457.

Pirkl, J. J. (1994). *Transgenerational design: Products for an aging population.* New York: Van Nostrand Reinhold.

Pirkl, J. J. (2011). Transgenerational design: A heart transplant for housing. In F. Kohlbacher & C. Herstatt (eds), *The silver market phenomenon: Business opportunities in an era of demographic change* (2nd ed., pp. 117–131). Heidelberg: Springer.

Pollay, R. W. (1986). The distorted mirror: Reflections on the unintended consequences of advertising. *Journal of Marketing, 50*(2), 18–36.

Praet, C. (1999). Characteristics of Japanese TV advertising: A review of the theoretical and empirical evidence. *Shōgakutōkyū, 50*(1), 151–179.

Praet, C. (2001). *Japanese advertising, the world's number one celebrity showcase? A cross-cultural comparison of the frequency of celebrity appearance in TV advertising.* Paper presented at the 2001 Special Asia–Pacific Conference of the American Academy of Advertising, Gainesville, FL.

Praet, C. (2009). National wealth or national culture? A multi-country study of the factors underlying the use of celebrity endorsement in television advertising. In P. De Pelsemacker & N. Dens (eds), *Advertising research: Message, medium, and context* (pp. 383–392). Antwerp: Garant.

Prieler, M. (2006a). Japanese advertising's foreign obsession. In P. Lutum (ed.), *Japanizing: The structure of culture and thinking in Japan* (pp. 239–271). Berlin: Lit-Verlag.

Prieler, M. (2006b). *The representation of "the Foreign" in Japanese television commercials*. Doctoral thesis, Tohoku University, Sendai, Japan.

Prieler, M. (2008a). Silver advertising: Elderly people in Japanese TV ads. In F. Kohlbacher & C. Herstatt (eds), *The silver market phenomenon: Business opportunities in an era of demographic change* (pp. 269–277). Heidelberg: Springer.

Prieler, M. (2008b). Specialities of Japanese television advertising. *Minikomi, 76*, 32–37.

Prieler, M. (2010). Othering, racial hierarchies and identity construction in Japanese television advertising. *International Journal of Cultural Studies, 13*(5), 511–529.

Prieler, M. (2012a). Gender representation in a Confucian society: South Korean television advertisements. *Asian Women, 28*(2), 1–26.

Prieler, M. (2012b). Social groups in South Korean television advertising: Foreigners and older people. *Keio Communication Review, 34*, 57–78.

Prieler, M., & Centeno, D. (2013). Gender representation in Philippine television advertisements. *Sex Roles, 69*(5/6), 276–288.

Prieler, M., Kohlbacher, F., Hagiwara, S., & Arima, A. (2009a). Ältere Menschen in der japanischen Fernsehwerbung: Eine umfragebasierte und inhaltsanalytische Untersuchung [Older people in Japanese television advertising: A survey and content-analysis-based study]. *Japanstudien, 21*, 197–222.

Prieler, M., Kohlbacher, F., Hagiwara, S., & Arima, A. (2009b). How older people are represented in Japanese TV commercials: A content analysis. *Keio Communication Review, 31*, 5–21.

Prieler, M., Kohlbacher, F., Hagiwara, S., & Arima, A. (2010). Older celebrity versus non-celebrity television advertising: A Japanese perspective. *Keio Communication Review, 32*, 5–23.

Prieler, M., Kohlbacher, F., Hagiwara, S., & Arima, A. (2011a). Gender representation of older people in Japanese television advertisements. *Sex Roles, 64*(5/6), 405–415.

Prieler, M., Kohlbacher, F., Hagiwara, S., & Arima, A. (2011b). Silver advertising: Older people in Japanese TV ads. In F. Kohlbacher & C. Herstatt (eds), *The silver market phenomenon: Marketing and innovation in the aging society* (2nd ed., pp. 239–247). Heidelberg: Springer.

Prieler, M., Kohlbacher, F., Hagiwara, S., & Arima, A. (2015). The representation of older people in television advertisements and social change: The case of Japan. *Ageing and Society, 35*(4), 865–887.

Rahtz, D. R., Sirgy, M. J., & Meadow, H. L. (1988). Elderly life satisfaction and television viewership: An exploratory study. *Advances in Consumer Research, 15*(1), 141–145.

Rahtz, D. R., Sirgy, M. J., & Meadow, H. L. (1989). The elderly audience: Correlates of television orientation. *Journal of Advertising, 18*(3), 9–20.

Ramaprasad, J., & Hasegawa, K. (1990). An analysis of Japanese television commercials. *Journalism Quarterly, 67*(4), 1025–1033.

Ramaprasad, J., & Hasegawa, K. (1992). Information content of American and Japanese television commercials. *Journalism Quarterly, 69*(3), 612–622.

Reinecke, J. A. (1964). The "older" market: Fact or fiction? *Journal of Marketing, 28*(1), 60–64.

Rentz, J. O., Reynolds, F. D., & Stout, R. G. (1983). Analyzing changing consumption patterns with cohort analysis. *Journal of Marketing Research, 20*(1), 12–20.

Richards, N., Warren, L., & Gott, M. (2012). The challenges of creating "alternative" images of ageing: Lessons from a project with older women. *Journal of Aging Studies, 26*(1), 65–78.

Richins, M. L. (1991). Social comparison and the idealized images of advertising. *Journal of Consumer Research, 18*(1), 71–83.

Riffe, D., Lacy, S., & Fico, F. G. (2005). *Analyzing media messages: Using quantitative content analysis in research.* Mahway: Lawrence Erlbaum.

Robinson, J. D., Skill, T., & Turner, J. W. (2004). Media usage patterns and portrayals of seniors. In J. F. Nussbaum & J. Coupland (eds), *Handbook of communication and aging research* (2nd ed., pp. 423–446). Mahwah: Lawrence Erlbaum Associates.

Robinson, T. (1998). *Portraying older people in advertising: Magazine, television, and newspapers.* New York: Garland.

Robinson, T., Gustafson, B., & Popovich, M. (2008). Perceptions of negative stereotypes of older people in magazine advertisements: Comparing the perceptions of older adults and college students. *Ageing & Society, 28*(2), 233–251.

Robinson, T., Popovich, M., Gustafson, R., & Fraser, C. (2003). Older adults' perceptions of offensive senior stereotypes in magazine advertisements: Results of a Q method analysis. *Educational Gerontology, 29*(6), 503–519.

Robinson, T., & Umphrey, D. (2006). First- and third-person perceptions of images of older people in advertising: An inter-generational evaluation. *International Journal of Aging and Human Development, 62*(2), 159–173.

Rotfeld, H. J., Reid, L. N., & Wilcox, G. B. (1982). Effect of age of models in print ads on evaluation of product and sponsor. *Journalism Quarterly, 59*(3), 374–381.

Roy, A., & Harwood, J. (1997). Underrepresented, positively portrayed: Older adults in television commercials. *Journal of Applied Communication Research, 25*(1), 39–56.

Russell, J. (1991). Race and reflexivity: The black other in contemporary Japanese mass culture. *Cultural Anthropology, 6*(1), 3–25.

Sasat, S., & Bowers, B. J. (2013). Spotlight Thailand. *The Gerontologist, 53*(5), 711–717.

Schiffman, L. G. (1971). Sources of information for the elderly. *Journal of Advertising Research, 11*(5), 33–37.

Schlaile, I. (2000). *Werbung in Japan – eine vergleichende Untersuchung kulturs-pezifischer Charakteristika der Werbung anhand von programmatischen Texten japanischer und westlicher Autoren (Setsuko Nakada, Guido Zurstiege u.a.) [Advertising in Japan – a comparative analysis of cultural specific characteristics of advertising based on programmatic texts of Japanese and Western authors (Setsuko Nakada, Guido Zurstiege and others].* Masters thesis, University of Munich, Munich.

Schmidt, S. J., & Spiess, B. (1994). Geschichte der Fernsehwerbung in der Bundesrepublik Deutschland: Eine Skizze [History of television advertising in the Federal Republic of Germany: An outline]. In H. D. Erlinger & H.-F. Foltin (eds), *Geschichte des Fernsehens in der Bundesrepublik Deutschland: Unterhaltung, Werbung und Zielgruppenprogramme* (vol. 4). Munich: Fink.

Schreiber, E. S., & Boyd, D. A. (1980). How the elderly perceive television commercials. *Journal of Communication, 30*(1), 61–70.

Sciglimpaglia, D., Lundstrom, W. J., & Vanier, D. J. (1979). Women's feminine role orientation and their attitudes toward sex role portrayals in advertising. *Current Issues & Research in Advertising, 2*(1), 163–175.

Sekizawa, H. (2008). The impact of the ageing of society on consumer behaviour and consumer markets. In F. Coulmas, H. Conrad, A. Schad-Seifert & G. Vogt (eds), *The demographic challenge: A handbook about Japan* (pp. 999–1016). Leiden: Brill.

Sherry, J. F. J., & Camargo, E. G. (1987). "May your life be marvelous": English language labelling and the semiotics of Japanese promotion. *Journal of Consumer Research, 14*(2), 174–188.

Shirahase, S. (2008). Income inequality in the ageing society. In F. Coulmas, H. Conrad, A. Schad-Seifert & G. Vogt (eds), *The demographic challenge: A handbook about Japan* (pp. 217–233). Leiden: Brill.

Shiraishi, N. (2008). Media use in the ageing society. In F. Coulmas, H. Conrad, A. Schad-Seifert & G. Vogt (eds), *The demographic challenge: A handbook about Japan* (pp. 513–530). Leiden: Brill.

Shrum, L. J., Burroughs, J. E., & Rindfleisch, A. (2005). Television's cultivation of material values. *Journal of Consumer Research, 32*(3), 473–479.

Shrum, L. J., Wyer, R. S., Jr., & O'Guinn, T. C. (1998). The effects of television consumption on social perceptions: The use of priming procedures to investigate psychological processes. *Journal of Consumer Research, 24*(4), 447–458.

Siano, A., Vollero, A., Confetto, M. G., & Sigliocolo, M. (2013). Corporate communication management: A framework based on decision-making with reference to communication resources. *Journal of Marketing Communications, 19*(3), 151–167.

Signorielli, N. (2004). Aging on television: Messages relating to gender, race, and occupation in prime time. *Journal of Broadcasting & Electronic Media, 48*(2), 279–301.

Signorielli, N., & Bacue, A. (1999). Recognition and respect: A content analysis of prime-time television characters across three decades. *Sex Roles, 40*(7/8), 527–544.

Simcock, P., & Sudbury, L. (2006). The invisible majority? Older models in UK television advertising. *International Journal of Advertising, 25*(1), 87–106.

Singh, S. N., & Cole, C. A. (1993). The effects of length, content, and repetition on television commercial effectiveness. *Journal of Marketing Research, 30*(1), 91–104.

Siu, W.-S., & Au, A. K.-M. (1997). Women in advertising: A comparison of television advertisements in China and Singapore. *Marketing Intelligence & Planning, 15*(5), 235–243.

Smith, R. B., & Moschis, G. P. (1985). A socialization perspective on selected consumer characteristics of the elderly. *The Journal of Consumer Affairs, 19*(1), 74–95.

Smith, R. B., Moschis, G. P., & Moore, R. L. (1984). Effects of advertising on the elderly consumer: An investigation of social breakdown theory. In R. W. Belk (ed.), *AMA Educators' Proceedings* (pp. 1–5). Chicago: American Marketing Association.

Smith, R. B., Moschis, G. P., & Moore, R. L. (1985). Some advertising influences on the elderly consumer: Implications for theoretical consideration. *Current Issues & Research in Advertising, 8*(2), 187–201.

Smythe, D. W. (1977). Communications: Blindspot of Western Marxism. *Canadian Journal of Political and Social Theory, 1*(3), 1–27.

Soeda, Y. (1978). Shutaiteki na ronenzō wo motomete [Toward the subjective image of the elderly]. *Gendai no Esprit, 126*, 5–24.

Sontag, S. (1972). The double standard of aging. *The Saturday Review, September 23*, 29–38.

Statistics Japan. (2013). Average monthly consumption expenditures per household. http://www.e-stat.go.jp/SG1/estat/XlsdlE.do?sinfid=000025408551

Statistics Japan. (2014a). Amounts of savings and liabilities held per household. http://www.e-stat.go.jp/SG1/estat/XlsdlE.do?sinfid=000029729288

Statistics Japan. (2014b). Population estimates. http://www.stat.go.jp/english/data/jinsui/2014np/index.htm

Stephens, N. (1991). Cognitive age: A useful concept for advertising? *Journal of Advertising, 20*(4), 37–48.

Stern, S. R., & Mastro, D. E. (2004). Gender portrayals across the life span: A content analytic look at broadcast commercials. *Mass Communication & Society, 7*(2), 215–236.

Stroud, D. (2005). *The 50-Plus Market: Why the future is age neutral when it comes to marketing & branding strategies*. London: Kogan Page.

Stroud, D., & Walker, K. (2013). *Marketing to the ageing consumer. The secrets to building an age-friendly business*. New York: Palgrave Macmillan.

Strutton, H. D., & Lumpkin, J. R. (1992). Information sources used by elderly health care product adopters. *Journal of Advertising Research, 32*(4), 20–30.

Sudbury, L., & Simcock, P. (2009a). A multivariate segmentation model of senior consumers. *Journal of Consumer Marketing, 26*(4), 251–262.

Sudbury, L., & Simcock, P. (2009b). Understanding older consumers through cognitive age and the list of values: A U.K.-based perspective. *Psychology & Marketing, 26*(1), 22–38.

Sudbury-Riley, L., & Idris, I. (2013). *Are advertisers finally waking up to the senior consumer? A content analysis of older adults in Malaysian advertising.* Paper presented at the British Academy of Management, Liverpool.

Sudbury-Riley, L., Kohlbacher, F., & Hofmeister, A. (2015). Baby boomers of different nations: Identifying horizontal international segments based on self-perceived age. *International Marketing Review, 32*(3/4), 245–278.

Sugimoto, Y. (2010). *An introduction to Japanese society* (3rd ed.). Cambridge: Cambridge University Press.

Suzuki, M. F. (1995). Women and television: Portrayal of women in the mass media. In K. Fujimura-Fanselow & A. Kameda (eds), *Japanese women: New feminist perspectives on the past, present, and future* (pp. 75–90). New York: Feminist Press.

Swayne, L. E., & Greco, A. J. (1987). The portrayal of older Americans in television commercials. *Journal of Advertising, 16*(1), 47–54.

Szmigin, I., & Carrigan, M. (2000a). Does advertising in the UK need older models? *Journal of Product & Brand Management, 9*(2), 128–143.

Szmigin, I., & Carrigan, M. (2000b). The older consumer as innovator: Does cognitive age hold the key? *Journal of Marketing Management, 16*(5), 505–527.

Taha, J., Sharit, J., & Czaja, S. (2009). Use of and satisfaction with sources of health information among older Internet users and nonusers. *The Gerontologist, 49*(5), 663–673.

Taylor, C. R., & Stern, B. B. (1997). Asian-Americans: Television advertising and the "model minority" stereotype. *Journal of Advertising, 26*(2), 47–61.

Tellis, G. J. (2004). *Effective advertising: Understanding when, how, and why advertising works.* Thousand Oaks: Sage.

Tréguer, J.-P. (2002). *50+ marketing: Marketing, communicating and selling to the over 50s generations.* Basingstoke: Palgrave.

Tse, D. K., Belk, R. W., & Zhou, N. (1989). Becoming a consumer society: A longitudinal and cross-cultural content analysis of print ads from Hong Kong, the People's Republic of China, and Taiwan. *Journal of Advertising, 15*(4), 457–472.

Tsuji, Y. (1997). Continuities and changes in the conceptions of old age in Japan. In S. Formanek & S. Linhart (eds), *Aging: Asian concepts and experiences – Past and present* (pp. 197–210). Vienna: Verlag der österreichischen Akademie der Wissenschaften.

United Nations Population Division. (2012). World Populations Prospects: The 2012 Revision. http://esa.un.org/wpp/unpp/panel_indicators.htm

Uray, N., & Burnaz, S. (2003). An analysis of the portrayal of gender roles in Turkish television advertisements. *Sex Roles, 48*(1/2), 77–87.

Ursic, A. C., Ursic, M. L., & Ursic, V. L. (1986). A longitudinal study of the use of the elderly in magazine advertising. *Journal of Consumer Research, 13*(1), 131–133.

Valls-Fernández, F., & Martínez-Vicente, J. M. (2007). Gender stereotypes in Spanish television commercials. *Sex Roles, 56*(9/10), 691–699.

Van Auken, S., & Barry, T. E. (2009). Assessing the nomological validity of a cognitive age segmentation of Japanese seniors. *Asia Pacific Journal of Marketing, 21*(3), 315–328.

Van Auken, S., Barry, T. E., & Bagozzi, R. P. (2006). A cross-country construct validation of cognitive age. *Journal of the Academy of Marketing Science, 34*(3), 439–455.

Wallander, K. (2013). Successful images of successful ageing? Representations of vigorous elderly people in a Swedish educational television programme. *Nordicom Review, 34*(1), 91–103.

WARC. (2014). Global ad trends 2013. http://www.warc.com/PDFFilesTmp/77646e18-fe98–46e8-b609–32f9908696f3.pdf

Webster, J. G., & Phalen, P. F. (1997). *The mass audience: Rediscovering the dominant model*. Mahwah: Lawrence Erlbaum Associates.

Westerhof, G. J., Harink, K., Van Selm, M., Strick, M., & Van Baaren, R. (2010). Filling a missing link: The influence of portrayals of older characters in television commercials on the memory performance of older adults. *Ageing & Society, 30*(5), 897–912.

Wheeler, S. C., & Petty, R. E. (2001). The effects of stereotype activation on behavior: A review of possible mechanisms. *Psychological Bulletin, 127*(6), 797–826.

Wolfe, D. B., & Snyder, R. E. (2003). *Ageless marketing: Strategies for reaching the hearts & minds of the new customer majority*. Chicago: Dearborn.

Yamada, M. (2005). *An analysis of Japanese TV commercials that feature foreign celebrities: A content analytic and interview approach*. Doctoral thesis, University of Oklahoma.

Yamada, Y. (1997). Quaker Oats. In Y. Yamada, M. Benson, K. Harimochi & S. Murakami (eds), *Culture, language, and advertising: Studies of Japanese and English advertisements* (pp. 63–85). Hiroshima: Hiroshima Shudo University.

Yamaki, T. (1994a). *Hikaku: Sekai no terebi CM [A comparison: International television commercials]*. Tokyo: Nikkei Kōkoku Kenkyūjo.

Yamaki, T. (1994b). *Kōkoku yōgo jiten [Advertising dictionary]*. Tokyo: Tōyō Keizai Shinpōsha.

Yamanaka, S. (2000). Nihon no terebi kōkoku ni okeru kōreishazō [The image of the elderly in Japanese television advertising]. *Kōkoku Kagaku, 40*(September), 61–75.

Ylänne, V. (2015). Representations of ageing in the media. In J. Twigg & W. Martin (eds), *Routledge Handbook of Cultural Gerontology* (pp. 369–376). Oxon: Routledge.

Ylänne, V. (ed.). (2012). *Representing ageing: Images and identities*. Basingstoke: Palgrave Macmillan.

Ylänne, V., & Williams, A. (2009). Positioning age: Focus group discussions about older people in TV advertising. *International Journal of the Sociology of Language 2009*(200), 171–187.

Yoon, H., & Powell, H. (2012). Older consumers and celebrity advertising. *Ageing & Society, 32*(8), 1319–1336.

Zandpour, F., Chang, C., & Catalano, J. (1992). Stories, symbols, and straight talk: A comparative analysis of French, Taiwanese, and U.S. TV commercials. *Journal of Advertising Research, 32*(1), 25–38.

Zhang, N. J., Guo, M., & Zheng, X. (2012). China: Awakening giant developing solutions to population aging. *The Gerontologist, 52*(5), 589–596.

Zhang, Y. B., Harwood, J., Ylänne-McEwen, V., Williams, A., Wadleigh, P. M., & Thimm, C. (2006). The portrayal of older adults in advertising: A cross-national review. *Journal of Language and Social Psychology, 25*(3), 264–282.

Zhang, Y. B., Song, Y., & Carver, L. J. (2008). Cultural values and aging in Chinese television commercials. *Journal of Asian Pacific Communication, 18*(2), 209–224.

Zhou, N., & Chen, M. Y. T. (1992). Marginal life after 49: A preliminary study of the portrayal of older people in Canadian consumer magazine advertising. *International Journal of Advertising, 11*(4), 343–354.

Zimmerman, L. L. (2001). *Television commercials and advertising approaches for the mature market: A content analysis.* Master Thesis, California State University, Long Beach.

Index

CPSIA information can be obtained
at www.ICGtesting.com
Printed in the USA
LVOW13*1428061216

516054LV00011B/354/P

DATE DUE	RETURNED